OCCASIONAL PAPER 83

Economic Reform in Hungary Since 1968

Anthony R. Boote and Janos Somogyi

INTERNATIONAL MONETARY FUND
Washington DC
July 1991

Library of Congress Cataloging-in-Publication Data

Boote, Anthony R.
Economic reform in Hungary since 1968 / by Anthony R. Boote and Janos Somogyi.
p. cm. — (Occasional paper, ISSN 0251-6365 ; 83)
"July 1991."
ISBN 1-55775-216-8 : $10.00
1. Hungary—Economic policy—1968–1989. 2. Hungary—Economic policy—1989– 3. Finance—Hungary. I. Somogyi, Janos. II. Title. III. Series: Occasional paper (International Moentary Fund) ; no. 83.
HC270.28.B66 1991
338.9439'009'09045—dc20 91-18827
CIP

Price: US$10.00
(US$7.50 to full-time faculty members and students at universities and colleges)

Please send orders to:
International Monetary Fund, Publication Services
700 19th Street, N.W., Washington, D.C. 20431, U.S.A.
Tel.: (202) 623-7430 Telefax: (202) 623-7201

Contents

The following symbols have been used throughout this paper:

... to indicate that data are not available;

— to indicate that the figure is zero or less than half the final digit shown, or that the item does not exist;

– between years or months (e.g., 1990–91 or January–June) to indicate the years or months covered, including the beginning and ending years or months;

/ between years (e.g., 1990/91) to indicate a crop or fiscal (financial) year.

"Billion" means a thousand million.

Minor discrepancies between constituent figures and totals are due to rounding.

The term "country," as used in this paper, does not in all cases refer to a territorial entity that is a state as understood by international law and practice; the term also covers some territorial entities that are not states, but for which statistical data are maintained and provided internationally on a separate and independent basis.

Preface

This paper is based on an internal report prepared in 1989 by Janos Somogyi. It has been revised and updated through March 1991 by Anthony R. Boote. Any opinions expressed are those of the authors and do not reflect the views of the Hungarian authorities (past or present), Executive Directors of the IMF, or IMF staff. The authors bear sole responsibility for any errors.

The authors gratefully acknowledge the assistance generously extended to them by the many officials with whom they worked during numerous visits to Budapest over the years. They would like to thank Gérard Bélanger, Balazs Horvath, George Kopits, Mark Lutz, and Tom Wolf for their valuable comments. Thanks are also due to the editor, David M. Cheney of the External Relations Department, to Valerie Asfour for assistance with charts, and to Patricia Emerson, Maria Lourdes Chuidian, and John Maynard for secretarial support.

I Introduction

Hungary was the first centrally planned economy to introduce a broad market-oriented reform, in 1968. It has been undertaking economic reforms ever since. And yet, the first freely elected government in forty years—which took office in May 1990—inherited a poorly performing, overcentralized economy with low external reserves and the highest per capita debt in Eastern Europe. What went wrong? This paper examines Hungary's experience with reform up to mid-1990, which is essential to understanding the reform measures recently introduced by the new Government and which may also be instructive for other formerly planned economies implementing their own reform programs.

Many positive elements emerge from a detailed review of Hungarian reforms between 1968 and mid-1990. The authorities implemented price reform early and avoided the major distortions common in other centrally planned economies. Queues were uncommon. Trade with western economies was significantly liberalized. Important institutional reforms were carried out in the areas of banking and taxation. In the 1980s, small private enterprises were the principal source of economic growth. The economy became more flexible and adaptable.

The overall results, however, were clearly unsatisfactory. The authorities continued to maintain substantial formal and informal central control. Reform measures were often partial, inconsistent, and subsequently reversed. The checkered history of wage regulation provides a classic example; the persistence of widespread enterprise tax allowances undermined the effectiveness of tax reform. The goal was to stimulate markets—such as by raising the administered price of raw materials to world market levels—rather than to provide scope for the interaction of market forces. There was a fundamental reluctance to permit competition between domestic enterprises and to close down chronic loss makers. The relationship between the State and state enterprises remained fatally flawed, and the representation of ownership interests remained unresolved in the dominant socialized sector of the economy. As Prime Minister Jozsef Antall stated in his inaugural address in May 1990, "In the economy, too, everything was upside down. The State embraced all activities in the direction and operation of the economy; the state enterprises were not real enterprises; state redistribution had pushed its way into the place of the market."

The State's domination of economic activity and its control over resource allocation reflected the fusion of economic and political power in the Hungarian Socialist Workers' Party. This fusion led many to conclude that political reform was necessary for the successful transformation of the economic system. As the Government stated in its March 1991 Program of Stabilization and Convertibility, "Political change and economic transformation: two processes that presuppose each other." The lesson of the Hungarian reform experience up to mid-1990 was, in the words of a senior official of the previous Government, that halfway does not work.

The new Government formed in mid-1990 has put in place a comprehensive reform program designed to complete the creation of the most important elements—including the institutional framework—of a contemporary market economy within three years. The Government, drawing on Hungary's earlier reform experience, is placing great emphasis on reducing the State's role in the economy through privatization and other measures, strengthening the operation of the free market, and developing an adequate social safety net.

The earliest example of a broad market-oriented reform program to be implemented in a centrally planned economy is Hungary's New Economic Mechanism (NEM), introduced in 1968. The NEM freed enterprises from mandatory plan directives and relaxed controls, which permitted a revival of small-scale cooperative and private activities. As a result, Hungary's economy improved in the first four to five years of the NEM, but not without the emergence of tensions. In particular, opposition to the decentralization of decision making proved to be stronger than anticipated, and contradictions between the requirements of the plan and the market appeared. The reform left intact most of the traditional institutional system of economic management. Moreover, it did not fundamentally alter the economic development strategy established during central planning.

After 1968, the authorities attempted periodically to improve the NEM and to rejuvenate the reform process. Although the system that evolved was no longer characterized by pervasive direct administrative controls, enterprises remained subject to informal direct controls; in addition, substantial indirect controls governed entry, exit, and the selection of lines of activity. The authorities were able to affect enterprises' financial results through price and wage regulations, taxes, and subsidies; throughout the period, they had a pervasive influence on enterprise activity. The instruments of indirect control were, however, applied with sufficient flexibility and supported by macroeconomic policies sufficiently balanced to avoid major disequilibria in the domestic economy, and especially chronic shortages and inflationary pressures in consumer markets. Macroeconomic policies were not sufficiently tight to avoid growing indebtedness vis-à-vis the convertible currency area and the frequent subordination of price and wage liberalization to anti-inflationary objectives.

One reason for inconsistencies in the reform process was that it foresaw the initiation of a fundamental reform of the institutional system only at a late stage. A key issue of institutional reform—the establishment of an effective representation of ownership interests in the state sector—was not resolved. This limited the extent to which management could be held accountable for the results of enterprise operations and the authorities could be freed from microeconomic responsibilities. These conditions tended to undermine financial discipline. They also complicated the enforcement of tight fiscal and monetary policies, which in turn limited the scope for further liberalization of the price and wage systems. The liberalization of private and small-scale cooperative economic activities, including in agriculture, contributed to a strengthening of supply. These operations, however, were frequently motivated mainly by a desire for quick results, given the past ambivalence of the authorities toward private undertakings.

Until recently, the scope and effectiveness of economic reform in Hungary were limited by the prevailing social-political model based on the Party's dominance of both political and economic activity. The omnipresence of the Party imposed limits on the reform blueprints and hampered their implementation. As a result, political reform was considered necessary for the successful transformation of the economic system. A crucial step in this direction was the conduct of the first free elections for more than forty years in March–April 1990. The coalition Government that assumed office in May 1990 has formulated a comprehensive program of economic reform aimed at moving to a market economy based on private ownership with a social safety net for the needy.

This paper describes the reform efforts undertaken prior to 1968, which were aimed at moving away from the traditional system of central planning through partial decentralization. It outlines the comprehensive blueprint of the NEM introduced in 1968. The paper then describes in detail the reforms undertaken between 1968 and mid-1990 with respect to (i) the system of macroeconomic decision making; (ii) the price system; (iii) the foreign trade and the exchange system; (iv) the wage system and labor market policies; (v) the fiscal system; (vi) the banking system and capital market; and (vii) agriculture. Each section concludes with an assessment of the position as of mid-1990 and with a summary of the new Government's subsequent policies and plans. Some of these reforms have benefited from IMF technical assistance since Hungary joined the IMF in 1982. This assistance has included advice on decentralizing the banking system; on developing monetary and credit policy instruments; on reforming the budgetary, tax, and social security systems; and on improving statistics.

The paper concludes with a review of recent economic developments and of the current economic situation in the context of the 1990 stand-by arrangement from the IMF. It outlines the Government's medium-term program, supported by an extended arrangement approved by the IMF's Executive Board in February 1991, as well as the Government's four-year Program of Stabilization and Convertibility unveiled in March 1991.

Hungary at a Glance

Population

Hungary is a relatively small country with a population of 10.5 million, which declined in the 1980s. Three fifths of the population lives in towns. The average life expectancy is seventy years.

Political System

From the late 1940s until 1990, political and economic power was monopolized by the Hungarian Socialist Workers' Party. Following the first free Parliamentary elections for forty years in the spring of 1990, a coalition government led by the Hungarian Democratic Forum assumed office.

Economy

Hungary's economic system is dominated by the state and cooperative sectors (the socialist sector), which accounted for 94 percent of gross domestic product (GDP) in 1988. The private sector, however, was the most dynamic sector in the 1980s. The economy is highly open: exports and imports together constitute about 80 percent of GDP. Until 1991, a major part of this trade was with partner countries of the Council for Mutual Economic Assistance (CMEA) at administered prices.

Past policies favoring extensive industrialization have transformed Hungary from an agricultural society to one in which industry accounted for about 35 percent of both GDP and employment in 1989. Almost all industry is in the socialist sector. Energy and basic materials accounted for approximately 20 percent of industrial production, with the remainder split between the manufacturing sub-sectors—machinery and engineering products, building materials, chemicals, light industry, and food processing.

Agriculture

Cooperatives own about three fifths of agricultural land, with some one quarter owned by state enterprises and one tenth by small-scale producers. Approximately one half of agricultural production derives from cooperatives, one sixth from state enterprises, and nearly two fifths from small-scale producers. About 18 percent of the labor force is engaged in agriculture and forestry. The major products are pork, wheat, corn, poultry, milk, beef, fruit, and vegetables.

Foreign Debt

Hungary has a relatively high convertible currency debt, equivalent to approximately three quarters of GDP. This largely reflects borrowing to finance domestic consumption associated with delayed adjustments to higher world prices, notably of energy and raw materials.

Selected Social and Demographic Indicators[1]

GDP per capita (current U.S. dollars)	2,781
External debt/GDP[2] (percent)	75
Area	
Total land area (sq. km.)	93,030
Agricultural land (in percent of total)	70
Forest and woodland (in percent of total)	18
Population and vital statistics	
Total population (in millions)	10.5
Urban population (in percent of total)	62
Population growth rate (annual percent)	–1.3
Population density (per sq. km.)	112
Population age structure (in percent)	
0–14 years	20
15–59 years	61
60 and above	19
Infant mortality rate (per thousand)	16
Life expectancy at birth (years)	70
Males	66
Females	74
Birth rate (per thousand)	11
Death rate (per thousand)	13
Labor force	
Total active labor force (in millions)	4.8
Participation rate (in percent)	46
In agriculture and forestry (in percent)	18
In industry (in percent)	30
Average monthly earnings (U.S. dollars)	
Gross	179
Net	138
Health and nutrition	
Proteins (grams per day)	106
Population per physician	287
Population per hospital bed	101
Housing	
Population per hundred dwellings	271
Owner occupied (in percent)	73
Dwellings with internal plumbing (in percent)	68
Education	
Enrollment rate (in percent)	
Primary	99
Secondary	76
Pupil-teacher ratio	
Primary	13
Other	
TV license holders (in percent)	28
Private cars (per thousand)	173
Telephones (per thousand)	167

Sources: Statistical Pocket Book of Hungary; Monthly Bulletin of Statistics; and IMF staff calculations.

[1] Estimates refer to the latest available year, generally 1989.

[2] Convertible currency, gross debt.

II Framework for Reform Since 1968

Central planning was introduced in Hungary in the late 1940s. It laid the basis for managing the economy after the authorities established the social ownership of the means of production through broad nationalization and, in agriculture, through widespread collectivization. Based on macroeconomic plans formulated at the center, basic production inputs were allocated directly and enterprises were fitted into the chain of command of central planning and management through specific and detailed directives concerning production, investment, employment, and the setting of wages and prices. The priority objective of rapid industrialization was pursued by imposing tight quantitative growth targets and forced saving, in an environment more or less insulated from the world economy. Rapid output growth was recorded as long as reserves of manpower, capital, and natural resources could be exploited. The process, however, involved high costs and major economic disequilibria, especially shortages of consumer goods.

The Government saw a need for major modifications at an early stage and took steps toward decentralization, accompanied by a relaxation of tight planning, a reduction in the number of compulsory plan indices, and wider latitude for prices in resource allocation. This process was interspersed with efforts to restore the dominant role of central planning and to suppress market elements. The authorities eventually came to recognize that the succession of partial measures had failed to resolve the problems with growth, the balance of payments in convertible currencies, and living standards. Against this background, in 1965, the Central Committee of the Hungarian Socialist Workers' Party commissioned a group of expert committees to draw up guidelines for a comprehensive reform. The leadership approved the recommendations in mid-1966, and the experts prepared the detailed decrees and regulations necessary to adopt the New Economic Mechanism (NEM) on January 1, 1968.

The New Economic Mechanism

The blueprint of the NEM outlined in the resolution of the Central Committee of the Party of May 7, 1966, represented a reform model aimed at modifying certain basic features of traditional central planning without overstepping the limits of the established social-political system. The objective was not to reform socialism but rather to improve the methods of "building socialism." The NEM blueprint preserved the basic principles of the system, including the dominance of social ownership of the means of production, the ideological postulates of socialism, and the central role of the national economic plan in the allocation of resources. The reform sought to bring about a more efficient implementation of the plan through market-based, decentralized decision making. It hoped to achieve consistency between the plan and market processes by replacing plan directives with indirect control via financial instruments. The reform blueprint also provided safeguards to protect the socialist character of the economy and to avoid "unhealthy excesses" of competition and "market anarchy."

The most important characteristic of the NEM was its elimination of directives and commands from the center. Correspondingly, it abolished the central allocation of the means of production and inputs and authorized trading among enterprises. The NEM recognized, however, the mixed nature of the economy. It envisioned a dominant role for the state sector, moderate scope for the private sector, and encouraged the expansion of the cooperative sector. Autonomous enterprises were to be responsible for microeconomic decision making subject to a uniformly applied system of economic regulations; the interests of employees were represented in the decision-making process of enterprises. Finally, the NEM plan envisaged a closer direct relationship between the domestic economy and foreign markets by introducing a unified exchange rate, a closer connection between domestic and foreign prices, and by licensing enterprises to engage directly in foreign trade.

The decentralization of decision making and the increase in enterprise autonomy were to be accompanied by a greater role for enterprise profits to guide production and marketing decisions, with more flexible prices intended to reflect the effects of supply and demand. The role of prices and wages in allocating resources was hampered by, among other things, a complex tax-subsidy structure that limited the effects of the reform on enterprise profitability. Moreover, price liberalization was introduced only gradually and the authorities did not foresee a significantly enhanced role for the exchange rate and interest rates as economic policy instruments. The banking system and various other aspects of the institutional system, such as the role of the government ministries, remained essentially unaffected by the reform.

The NEM was never intended to replace planning by the market but rather to implement the planner's priorities through market-based incentives. The substantial prerogatives remaining with the planners were frequently used to subvert the market's influence. The result was a set of conflicting signals that precluded fundamental economic change. Enterprises switched from bargaining with the center about the plan to bargaining about regulations.

III Reform of Microeconomic Decision Making

As part of the 1968 economic reforms, the central authorities lost the power to set physical output targets for individual enterprises and abolished the centralized allocation of materials. Enterprises were expected to evolve into autonomous entrepreneurial units responding to market signals and to uniformly applied macroeconomic policy measures. The latter measures—implemented through laws, decrees, guidelines, and financial incentives—were designed to serve as instruments of indirect control for achieving the priorities set out in national economic plans.

The institutional relationships of enterprises to their supervisory agencies—mostly ministries or local authorities—and the methods of appointment, evaluation, and remuneration of managers, however, were not fundamentally changed. Enterprises remained subject to the formal and informal interference of government supervisors and representatives of social and political organizations. In particular, in 1972 the Government reversed reforms by decreeing a large wage rise for Hungarian workers. The State Enterprise Act of 1977 sought to strike a better balance between centralized control and state enterprise autonomy by loosening the ties of enterprises to their supervisory agencies. The act established a legal framework for the creation of supervisory boards for trusts and conglomerates, which would assume part of the supervisory functions of the central authorities. The boards were organs of the supervisory state bodies, which appointed their members. The State Enterprise Act of 1977 also allowed the optional establishment of boards of directors in large enterprises. The boards were entitled to make strategic decisions concerning the future of the firm, while current operational decisions remained the prerogative of the enterprise's director. In order to reduce further the scope for formal and informal outside intervention in enterprise activities, the authorities, in January 1981, merged the three industrial branch ministries into a single Ministry of Industry and transferred their marketing and price-setting prerogatives to the National Materials and Price Board. They also modified, in 1981 and 1982, regulations concerning the selection of top managers and the appointment of senior staff in enterprises to encourage the appointment of company directors for fixed terms on the basis of open tenders.

These measures were nevertheless insufficient to resolve the ambivalent relationship between the central authorities and state enterprises. They did not succeed in severing the vertical ties between enterprises and supervisory authorities. Moreover, the discretionary reallocation of resources based on a heavy reliance on a differential system of taxes and subsidies and centralized allocation of credits—which validated central priorities and accommodated the lack of financial discipline at the enterprise level—remained essentially unchanged.

Amendments to the State Enterprise Act of 1977 and other legislation, which took effect January 1, 1985, established a new institutional framework for state enterprises—excluding trusts, public utilities, defense-related industries, and other selected large companies—based on self-management with workers' participation. The State retained the right to establish and own state enterprises and to supervise the legality of their activities. In large state companies, basic decisions over production, marketing, investment, organization, and mergers, and over the creation of subsidiaries, however, were delegated to enterprise councils—representing employees and managerial staff; in small enterprises of up to five hundred employees, these decisions were delegated to the assembly of employees, with a role secured in the new supervisory organs for representatives of the enterprises' party, youth, and trade union organizations. Responsibility for current operations resided with the chief executive elected by the enterprise council or assembly for fixed-term appointments of up to five years. Candidates were vetted by the regional party organization, and the sponsoring government authority could veto the appointment but not present its own candidate. The enterprise councils and assemblies could also decide on the performance criteria and remuneration of managers. By the latter part of 1987, about 73 percent of state enterprises had been transformed in this fashion and were under the supervision of enterprise councils or assemblies; 27 percent—more than one half representing public utilities—remained under direct state control. To guard against excessive wage payments, the premia of managers—which accounted for 40–60 percent of their remuneration—were linked to the profitability of the enterprise and were subject to cuts if wage growth outpaced that of the value added of the enterprise.

With a relaxation of fiscal and monetary policies in 1985 and 1986, macroeconomic imbalances became an increasing source of concern. Tax-based wage controls were consequently tightened and the rules requiring prior notification by enterprises of contemplated price adjustments were enforced more strictly, which limited the decision-making authority of enterprises.

The poor performance of state enterprises resulted largely from interference by the central authorities. It also reflected the lack of effective exercise of ownership rights in state enterprises. The Law on Transformation adopted in June 1989 sought to provide the legal framework for transforming state enterprises and cooperatives into joint stock companies. It also allowed for the transfer of ownership in part or whole to foreign investors. However, the law did not remove the ambiguity in ownership rights. This continued ambiguity—and the interaction of the Enterprise Law and the Law of Association—permitted enterprise managers to abuse the transformation process. To check these abuses, Parliament approved legislation establishing a State Property Agency (SPA) in January 1990 and appointed a managing director in February. Subsequently, Parliament decided to make the Agency responsible to government. It also adopted legislation to establish a mechanism to control enterprise-initiated privatizations to ensure that the process was transparent and fair.

The new Government sees a pivotal task for privatization in reducing the State's role in the economy. Its goal is to reduce the share of state-owned property to less than half of total assets in the competitive sphere of the economy by 1993. Privatization will be accomplished through three main channels. Retail shops and restaurants are being auctioned to private owners through the preprivatization program, which was approved by Parliament in September 1990. The SPA will launch active privatization programs for the sale of large enterprises, with privatization managers—often western experts—selected through a tender process. By the end of 1990, two such programs—each involving about twenty enterprises—were initiated. Privatization initiated by the enterprise itself or by a potential buyer will be encouraged, with the SPA role limited to ensuring that the enterprise is appropriately valued and that the process is transparent. The emphasis will be on achieving privatization through market means. Partial compensation will be provided to former owners of property nationalized under the past regime. The Government, in its four-year program launched in March 1991, proposes to accelerate privatization by drawing up a national privatization strategy, streamlining the State Property Agency, and decentralizing the process.

The Government recognizes that foreign investment brings not only much needed financial resources, but also modern management methods, modern technology, and better market access. It plans to encourage foreign investment; in 1991, only the five largest banks and enterprises with monopolistic positions were ineligible for foreign investment. The regulations governing the foreign acquisition of property and real estate will be gradually liberalized. Direct foreign investment rose sharply in 1990 (see Section X).

The Government intends to strengthen financial discipline and management for enterprises remaining within the state sector. It is also preparing a new accounting and auditing law—to be implemented at the beginning of 1992—to bring Hungarian accounting procedures in line with recognized international standards.

Financial Discipline and Bankruptcy Provisions

In 1983, new regulations took effect to accelerate the phasing-out of inefficient enterprises. The regulations provided that loss-making enterprises draw up restructuring programs aimed at eliminating losses. If this were not done, the supervisory authorities could order a withdrawal of capital and labor resources, a replacement of managers, forced restructuring, or, as a last resort, liquidation of the enterprise. These regulations, however, were rarely invoked.

In the mid-1980s, the authorities took new initiatives to foster financial responsibility and economic efficiency among unprofitable enterprises. In 1986, new multiyear restructuring plans were adopted for the ferrous metallurgy and coal mining industries, which had been in chronic financial difficulty, and the authorities developed a program to restructure the construction sector. Also, in September 1986, a new bankruptcy law provided a legal framework for restructuring or closing inefficient enterprises. This framework relied primarily on negotiations between creditors and debtors for an out-of-court settlement of claims. If settlement were not reached, a State Restructuring Institution—under the auspices of the Ministry of Finance—determined within thirty days whether restructuring of the ailing enterprise warranted state support through a refloatation agreement on account of regional employment, national defense considerations, or to meet international obligations (mostly stemming from trade agreements with Council for Mutual Economic Assistance (CMEA) partner countries). As a last resort, creditors could turn to the courts to initiate bankruptcy proceedings. After the enterprise was declared bankrupt, its assets were liquidated under the supervision of the State Restructuring Institution. The proceeds were used to cover the cost of the proceedings and to satisfy to the extent possible all claims on the bankrupt enterprise, with priority given to settling wages and other employee claims.

Until 1989, the provisions of the bankruptcy law were largely used to liquidate small enterprises on a modest scale. Creditors were reluctant to initiate bankruptcy proceedings against large, chronic loss makers that might be their principal or sole customers. Banks were also reluctant to absorb such losses (see Section VIII). Nonviable and illiquid enterprises continued to operate by not paying their creditors (mainly other enterprises and commercial banks).

In December 1989, the Government reached agreement with the three major commercial banks to accelerate the process of liquidation; the Government gave up the option of "refloating" targeted loss-making companies and commercial banks were free to initiate appropriate procedures against debtors judged not to be creditworthy on commercial criteria. Banks were permitted to use part of their blocked risk reserves to write off resulting bad debts. As a result of this agreement, some forty enterprises were instructed to repay outstanding loans or develop restructuring plans approved by the banks; the restructurings involved asset sales, management changes, and staff reductions. About one quarter of the enterprises repaid their outstanding loans or developed approved restructuring plans; the remainder was subject to liquidation proceedings. In addition, the authorities took action against enterprises with tax arrears. Proceedings were also initiated independently by creditors against some well-known large companies, and restructuring plans involving foreign investors were drawn up.

An amendment to the bankruptcy law, effective May 1, 1990, provided for compulsory self-liquidation of state enterprises with net payments arrears, with penalties against enterprise directors for noncompliance. During 1990, liquidation procedures were initiated against more than four hundred enterprises.

The new Government recognizes that the transformation of the Hungarian economy into a modern market economy requires the restructuring or elimination of loss-making enterprises. It will formulate a new bankruptcy act aimed at shortening the liquidation process. Bankruptcy proceedings will be initiated against any enterprise with tax or social security contribution arrears of more than three months. The Government has also taken steps to increase the number of courts competent to deal with bankruptcy cases and to simplify procedures. Stronger prudential regulation (see Section VIII) should discourage banks from lending to loss-making enterprises. The Government has begun implementing a plan to improve the efficiency of the construction sector, including privatization of large state companies and support for private companies.

Promotion of Competition and the Private Sector

The industrialization of the postwar period entailed heavy industrial concentration to promote central control and large-scale production. The result of successive mergers was a virtual absence of small- and medium-sized enterprises in the socialized sector; the share of industrial employment in enterprises of up to fifty employees was only 0.1 percent in 1980. A review of concentration in 1979 concluded that it inhibited competition, hampered progress toward greater enterprise autonomy, and explained much of the sluggishness in the structural adaptation of industry. Subsequently, the authorities launched a process of decentralization, which involved the dismantling of a number of trusts and conglomerates.

During most of the period under review, the main activity laid down in an enterprise's founding charter could be modified only upon approval by the founding organization and branch ministry. More flexible rules were introduced in 1982 and 1983. These rules permitted enterprises to engage in other than their main line of activity for up to 30 percent of their output; removed the territorial and sectoral constraints on the activities of trading companies; and permitted retail traders to deal directly with producers. In early 1985, the authorities abolished the distinction between an enterprise's main line of activity and its ancillary operations and shifted the prerogative to determine the enterprise's lines of activity to the enterprise council or staff assembly and management. In January 1986, the "profile restrictions" of specialized foreign trade companies were eased and their monopoly positions ended.

At the start of 1982, new legal rules took effect to promote the creation and expansion of small- and medium-sized enterprises in the socialized sector; to legalize activities in the second economy; and to open opportunities for new private sector undertakings (Chart 1). These rules helped achieve remarkable success in improving the supply of goods and services. In the state enterprise sector, the new legislation provided scope for establishing independent small companies and subsidiaries of existing firms, transferring facilities of state enterprises to private operators, and organizing partnerships among the staff (so-called "enterprise economic partnerships"). The members of these partnerships operated the equipment of the enterprise on their own time to perform specific tasks that, together with their separate remuneration, were contractually agreed with management. New enterprise forms—including independent economic partnerships and civil law companies—were also permitted in the cooperative and private sectors.

On the whole, the impact of the rapid growth of the private sector on the competitive environment up to 1988 remained limited; the most rapid expansion occurred through economic partnerships of employees in socialized enterprises in activities that complemented goods and services produced by those enterprises. Also, despite steps to liberalize foreign trading rights, foreign trade had only a moderate effect on competition, as import licensing was used to encourage potential importers to give preference to domestic suppliers.

Chart 1. Breakdown of GDP by Social Sector[1]

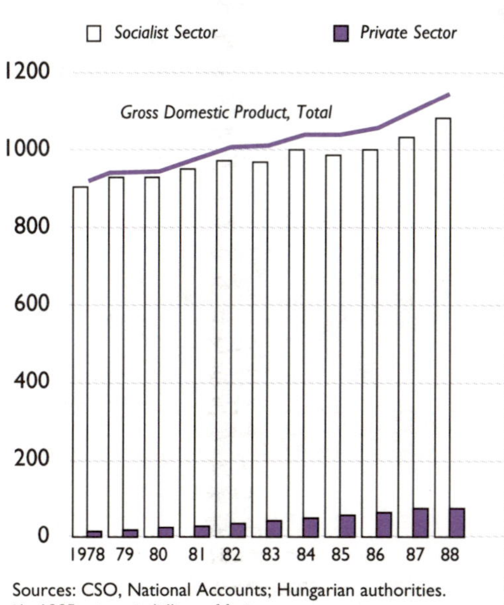

Sources: CSO, National Accounts; Hungarian authorities.
[1] In 1985 prices, in billion of forints.

Against this background, the authorities took new steps in early 1989 aimed at corporate reform and import liberalization. The new corporate association law and complementary legislation allowed great freedom for resident and nonresident individuals and legal entities to establish and participate in a variety of corporate entities suited to their purposes; these included unlimited liability companies, silent partnerships, limited liability companies, and joint ventures with a limited liability, as well as joint stock companies. The law permitted individuals to acquire shares in enterprises with the State as the majority shareholder; it also authorized private enterprises to expand to five hundred employees (from thirty). The legislation also established more liberal rules for joint ventures with foreign partners, requiring government approval only in the case of a majority share or full ownership by the foreign investor.

These measures led to the registration of 4,578 new enterprises in 1989, compared with 1,377 in 1988. In 1990, the authorities abolished the employment limit on private businesses. They also adopted a comprehensive program to encourage new ventures; this program provided for accelerated depreciation for investment in marketing and equipment, credit facilities, creation of investment companies, and improved access to supporting infrastructure services. Also in early 1990, the authorities established a deregulation law establishing a deregulation board reporting directly to the prime minister. The aim was to repeal unnecessary regulations—notably those discouraging the entry of new businesses.

Until recently, progress toward effective institutional reform and structural transformation of the economy was limited, notwithstanding the initiatives undertaken to modify the organization of state enterprises and legislative actions that would provide a liberal environment for the operation of enterprises. This was partly the result of the dominance of short-term priorities promoting the basic materials industries in production and in convertible currency exports. Ownership rights over state enterprises were not effectively exercised. This reflected ambivalence by the State over whether these rights should be exercised at the enterprise level by managements or some self-governing body or should remain centralized. The result was weakened financial discipline and an undermining of managers' interest in the most efficient allocation of the resources at their disposal. This in turn justified the continued interference of supervisory bodies in microeconomic decisions. Finally, the implementation of restructuring programs was hampered by systemic and policy constraints that encouraged the avoidance of the consequences of restructuring, in terms of changing the composition of output and exports, reallocating labor, and writing off capital.

The new Government is determined to tackle this legacy. It sees the transfer of state property to the private sector as a main means of resolving the unsatisfactory relationship between the State and state enterprises. The Government is determined to achieve a major breakthrough in privatization over the next three years. It also wishes to foster the growth of private property through the active promotion of new enterprises. It continues to provide tax incentives—such as accelerated depreciation for investment in machinery and equipment—to the private sector. And the authorities plan to encourage private sector access to credit by restricting credit demands by the budget and large state enterprises. Legislation is planned for 1991 to promote the flow of venture capital.

The Government wants to enhance the spirit of enterprise by both deregulating the Hungarian economy and promoting competition. It will continue to relax or eliminate restrictions. And it implemented a new law prohibiting unfair market practices at the start of 1991. The law establishes a Cartel Office to investigate complaints of monopolistic and noncompetitive behavior and to monitor mergers and acquisitions. The Cartel Office will implement an effective anti-trust policy that sends a strong signal to business that competitive, efficiency-enhancing behavior is acceptable and that conversely, monopolizing, rent-seeking behavior is unacceptable. The Cartel Office will take action to break up existing monopolies, such as in the domestic trade sector.

IV Price Reform

Before the introduction of the New Economic Mechanism in 1968, prices were generally fixed by the authorities and did not reflect the relative scarcity of resources. Differentials between foreign and domestic prices were compensated by transfers of special funds, and consumer and producer prices were separated through a complex system of turnover taxes and subsidies. The 1968 reform introduced a three-tiered price system:

- fixed prices set by the Government;
- flexible prices, allowed to fluctuate between officially set upper and lower limits; and
- so-called free prices set by enterprises according to predetermined rules.

The new regulations foresaw a greater freedom for enterprises to set prices in response to market forces, but even the free prices remained subject to considerable administrative control. Specific rules governed cost calculations and admissible profit margins and required prior notification of intended price increases on specified products. The National Materials and Price Office also intervened directly to prevent price increases it deemed excessive.

In addition, regulations concerning the profitability of enterprises affected the extent to which producer price adjustments could be passed on to customers or had to be absorbed by profits. This led to a compression of differentials in profitability. Moreover, as a result of an active policy of exchange rate appreciation aimed at moderating the impact of foreign price increases on domestic inflation, the commercial exchange rate fell below the level at which the average cost of earning a unit of foreign currency in exports could be covered. This prompted exporters to press for special assistance, which took the form of special tax exemptions and subsidies.

The Government did not undertake renewed price reform until 1979–80, after it recognized that allocative distortions and economic disequilibria had become unsustainable. First, consumer prices were raised substantially in mid-1979, both to curb consumer demand and to encourage a shift of resources to the external sector. The authorities reduced net food subsidies and raised the net taxation of luxury goods through cuts in price subsidies and changes in turnover tax rates. Despite marked increases in prices of household energy, the subsidy content nevertheless increased because of rises in import and producer prices. The prices of services, including rent and transportation, were not adjusted, and subsidies on these items continued to rise. Second, domestic prices of energy and raw materials were linked to world market prices. The difference between domestic prices and prices of imported inputs from the CMEA area was bridged through "producers' differential turnover taxes." In the absence of significant competition, the authorities established a "competitive" price system—intended to simulate competitive price determination. Under this system, domestic prices and profit margins were constrained by the development of export prices and export profit margins. Domestic prices of individual products could not exceed prices of comparable imports by more than could be justified by quality differentials. The National Materials and Price Office monitored and enforced these complex rules (Charts 2 and 3).

Whereas the competitive pricing scheme in the manufacturing sector gave firms an incentive to improve the composition of exports to the convertible currency area, it was also criticized for restraining the real growth of such exports. Enterprises were able to raise profit margins on domestic sales and on exports to the ruble area by reducing the volume of sales to convertible currency markets and by eliminating altogether their less profitable exports. The authorities consequently introduced several modifications that relaxed the mechanical linkage of domestic price formation to foreign price developments.

Beginning in 1985, enterprises that could prove that a substantial part of their output could be exported at a profit—and that did not dominate the domestic market—were eligible to join a so-called price club. Members of this club were freed from the pricing rules limiting profit margins and price increases on domestic sales to export price developments, but they remained subject to the

Chart 2. Distribution of Consumer Prices by Pricing Category
(In percent of total)

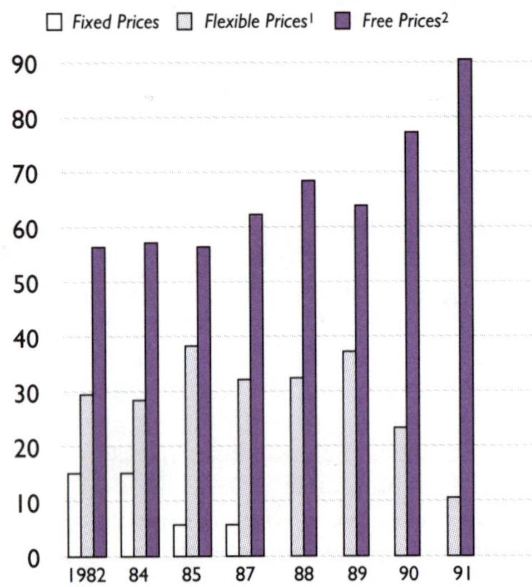

Source: Hungarian authorities.
[1]Includes prices subject to a maximum limit.
[2]Free prices, until 1991, not allowed to exceed prices of comparable imports.

Chart 3. Distribution of Producer Prices by Pricing Category
(In percent of total)

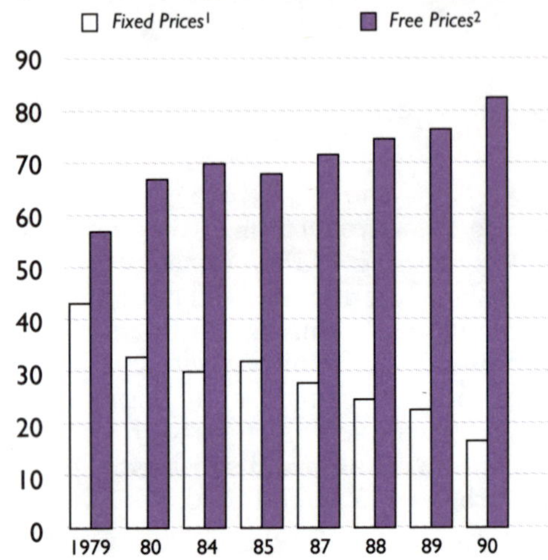

Source: Hungarian authorities.
[1]Includes fixed prices, prices fluctuating between officially set lower and upper limits, and prices subject to a maximum limit.
[2]Free prices not allowed to exceed prices of comparable imports.

import price constraint. A law against unfair trade practices was adopted in 1985, to provide safeguards against price distortions stemming from an abuse of market power. The law foresaw a shift of prerogatives for the enforcement of fair pricing behavior from administrative bodies to the courts. Because of the dominant influence of administrative bodies, however, these changes were not effectively implemented.

The pricing rules were increasingly perceived to interfere with the promotion of convertible currency exports and import substitution, and the authorities abolished the competitive pricing system in the manufacturing sector in March 1987. Moreover, the restrictive application of the rule prohibiting "unfair" profits, which was seen as an obstacle to raising domestic prices to the level of import prices, was relaxed at midyear. Still, the import price constraint remained in force. The authorities also continued to issue policy guidelines limiting price increases for groups of products—with which enterprises were expected to conform—and to monitor closely the price policy of enterprises.

At the beginning of 1988, producer prices were realigned in connection with the introduction of a personal income tax and the associated grossing up of wages. In addition, strongly differentiated turnover taxes were replaced by a less differentiated value-added tax (VAT), and subsidies were cut. As a result, agricultural and food prices increased and prices in manufacturing, construction, and the services sectors declined. The streamlining of turnover tax rates and subsidy cuts also led to a marked rise in consumer prices. Whereas the price club was discontinued, the authorities introduced a price consultation process with enterprises in areas where market disturbances were anticipated—for example, where market shares of individual suppliers exceeded 25 percent, or where supply difficulties or exceptional price increases occurred. On April 1, 1988—when the general application of the advance notification of intended price increases expired—20 percent of consumer prices remained subject to administratively set ceilings, 22 percent to the advance reporting obligation, and 5 percent to the price consultation process. The remaining 53 percent were subject only to the import price limitation and other general pricing rules that ensure compliance with the law against unfair trade practices. The share of free prices in this sense was raised to 62.5 percent from the beginning of 1989 and to 77 percent at the start of 1990; at the same time, the authorities eliminated the category of price consultations and freed certain agricultural prices.

As a result of the repeated efforts since the 1950s to overhaul the price system, Hungary avoided the accumulation of major distortions in relative prices that characterized most centrally planned economies. The administrative price realignments adopted by the authorities, the linkage of raw materials and energy prices to world market prices, and the adoption of rules to allow greater flexibility in the price policy of enterprises all played a significant role. However, the pricing rules constrained only the profit margins, and not the production costs, of enterprises. At the same time, the remaining administrative controls and the close monitoring of free price formation (an important instrument of anti-inflationary policy) slowed the adjustment of prices to market conditions. Moreover, price distortions attributable to the system of differentiated taxes and subsidies continued to interfere with a rational allocation of resources. Adverse consequences of the latter policies were visible particularly in the excessive weight of heavy industry in production and exports, and in the imbalances in the housing, energy, pharmaceuticals, and health services markets.

The new Government recognizes the need to increase competition through the liberalization of goods and factor markets to create the proper conditions for structural change and efficient resource use. It has taken further steps to liberalize prices. From the beginning of 1991, with the majority of domestic producers subject to competition from imports, the share of consumer prices free from controls was raised to about 90 percent. Central control of prices remains only for textbooks, one type of milk, white bread, and public utilities; local governments set local transport tariffs and housing rents on government-owned flats. Prices liberalized in January 1991 included retail prices of gasoline and fuel oil, while other energy prices were raised substantially. Producer prices for coal, wood for heating, electricity, and natural gas remain controlled. The Price Office, which was responsible for controlling prices, was abolished in January 1991. The rule limiting domestic prices to the price of comparable imports was also abolished. The Government took steps to reduce the scope of production and consumption subsidies and tax allowances (see Section VII). The Government plans to liberalize further regulations on prices. Price liberalization will be reinforced by the stronger competitive environment resulting from import liberalization, the law prohibiting unfair market practices, and the strengthening of enterprise financial discipline.

V Foreign Trade and Exchange Rate Reform

Hungary's foreign trade system consisted until 1991 of two separate regimes of approximately equal importance in terms of the volume of trade: one with market economies and one with the socialist world. Reform of the trade system focused on the regime governing trade with market economies. The system governing trade with the socialist world—especially with other CMEA members—remained relatively unchanged until the introduction of trade at world market prices in 1991.

Trade with Market Economies

The state monopoly of foreign trade, instituted in 1948, remained intact after the 1968 economic reform, with commercial exports and imports continuing to be carried out by authorized state-owned economic organizations. The state-owned entities included specialized foreign trade organizations and domestic producers and trading companies, with a general or specific permit to engage in foreign trade transactions on their own account or on a commission basis. The authorities took major steps toward more liberal foreign trading rights in 1981, when the role of "parallel" foreign trade transactions—allowing different foreign trade organizations to trade a particular product—was expanded, and in 1986, when the authorities made more flexible the approval process for applications and widened the scope for general export and import rights. In mid-1987, the authorities extended general foreign trading rights to any enterprise in the socialized sector whose convertible currency exports amounted to at least $1 million in the previous year. Such enterprises could export and import any product not specified in negative lists, while other enterprises with foreign trading rights could export their own products and import inputs needed for their own activities.

A further major change, which ended the system of foreign trade as a state monopoly, was introduced at the beginning of 1988. Under the new regime, every organization registering with the Ministry of Trade, including private entities, was authorized to engage in commercial foreign trade transactions without prior application and approval. The registration was automatic at the request of the enterprise and upon a declaration that certain organizational and personnel conditions were fulfilled. As a result, the number of enterprises authorized to engage in foreign trade increased to more than two thousand in 1989 from three hundred and fifty in 1986. Registered companies were entitled to trade any product not included in negative lists of exports and imports, whose trade required formal authorization. The negative list was reduced to 36 percent of convertible currency exports at the beginning of 1989. The authorities maintained the list to monitor the compliance of exporters with voluntary export restraint agreements and to regulate exports of farm products to meet the requirements of the European Community (EC). At the same time, the negative list of trading rights for imports was reduced to 20 percent of convertible currency imports. These lists were reduced further in 1990.

In addition, all exports and imports were subject to a licensing requirement, designed mainly to ensure that only authorized entities engaged in foreign trade. No export controls were applied to ensure adequate domestic supplies or for trade policy purposes. Apart from imports of consumer goods, which were subject to a global quota, most import licensing was semi-automatic, with the pace of processing and the issuance of licenses influenced periodically by balance of payments considerations. The value of the import quota for consumer goods was published annually, and licenses against the quota were issued on an order-of-arrival basis.

The authorities took an important step toward liberalizing imports vis-à-vis the convertible currency area at the beginning of 1989. They lifted the licensing requirement for products included in a positive list and reduced the coverage of the consumer goods quota; these measures affected about 40 percent of convertible currency imports, competing with an estimated 16 percent of domestic industrial production (excluding energy). In 1990, the share of convertible currency imports free from quota or licensing restrictions was raised to 65 percent of total imports, competing with around 30 percent of domestic industrial production. In addition, the quota on imports of consumer goods was increased by 30 percent to $250 million.

The new Government plans to construct a modern European social market economy integrated into the world economy. It aims to become part of the European economic region in the fullest possible sense. Linking Hungary's economy to Europe will be furthered by gradually adjusting taxes, customs duties, standards, and quality control to European norms. The Government recognizes the positive role of imports for quality improvements and competitiveness. It introduced further major liberalization beginning in 1991. The share of liberalized imports was increased to about 90 percent of total imports, exposing fully to foreign competition approximately 70 percent of industrial production. The consumer goods quota was increased to $630 million, and the coverage of the quota was reduced to those goods requiring import licensing (mainly processed foods and clothing). The licensing requirement was shifted from a positive list to a negative list consisting mainly of products requiring licensing for health and safety reasons (such as drugs and weapons), textiles, leather, certain chemicals, telecommunication equipment, and agricultural products. With the liberalization of trading rights, the number of agents with general trading rights is estimated to triple in 1991, from the 1990 level of ten thousand. The Government is committed to further import liberalization, which it will implement in the context of multilateral negotiations with General Agreement on Tariffs and Trade (GATT) partners. The Government expects to conclude an association agreement with the European Community in 1992.

Trade with the Ruble Area

Until the end of 1990, the bulk of Hungary's trade with the ruble area was conducted under bilateral quotas negotiated in annual official trade agreements. These agreements ensured essential imports of energy and raw materials, against which the Government committed to export Hungarian agricultural and industrial products. In this market, Hungarian enterprises faced a sizable volume of demand, which promoted economies of scale and involved requirements concerning quality, packaging, punctual delivery, and servicing of products less stringent than in the convertible currency or domestic markets. Bilateral balances arising from transactions with a particular CMEA partner country could not be used to settle imbalances with other CMEA countries.

Pricing rules guiding intra-CMEA trade changed over the years, from fixed prices in the 1950s, to an adjustment of prices at five-year intervals in the 1960s and early 1970s; and since the mid-1970s, to annual adjustments based on moving five-year averages of world market prices according to the "Bucharest formula." These rules were combined in practice, however, with extensive bargaining over technical aspects, rebates, discounts, and payment terms. As CMEA foreign trade prices remained distorted relative to world market prices, the Hungarian authorities applied a system of taxes and subsidies to ensure that enterprises achieved similar profitability in ruble trade transactions as in trade with convertible currency and domestic partners. On the import side, so-called producers' differential turnover taxes were generally applied, whereas on the export side, predominantly subsidies were paid to enterprises. Under this system, adjustments in the exchange rate of the forint vis-à-vis the transferable ruble were less important for influencing the attractiveness of ruble trade transactions than for determining the volume of transfers between the budget and enterprises engaged in ruble trade operations.

Until the beginning of 1988, enterprises received full and automatic compensation from the budget for the difference between the profitability of transactions with convertible currency or domestic customers and the profitability of ruble trade based on their own calculations of the amounts to which they claimed to be entitled. The system of guaranteed profitability allowed enterprises broad scope for budgetary support by shifting overhead costs to ruble exports. For ruble exports under the bilateral quotas considered essential to ensuring priority energy and raw materials imports, enterprises were in a particularly strong position to make the fulfillment of the ruble export contracts contingent on favorable guaranteed profit rates.

At the beginning of 1988, the Government acted to tighten the loose financial discipline inherent in ruble trade regulations. The method of self-assessment was replaced by a system under which the rate of budgetary compensation was set in advance for the subsequent year for every enterprise. In response to the surging ruble trade surplus in 1989, which undermined the effectiveness of domestic monetary policy, further measures were taken to curb ruble exports. The forint was appreciated by 5.5 percent vis-à-vis the transferable ruble to Ft 27.5 = TR 1 from September 1, 1989; some export licenses were canceled and a new settlement system for above-quota exports was introduced. Effective October 1, the National Bank of Hungary (NBH) stopped encashing into forints transferable rubles earned on above-quota exports, with such rubles instead freely traded with other enterprises wishing to import outside the quota system. The forint traded in this market at a premium of 25–30 percent. Following a substantial trade surplus early in 1990, the authorities withdrew CMEA export licenses and began issuing licenses monthly, and subsequently quarterly, in light of trade developments.

Events in 1989 and in early 1990 underlined the obstacles posed by the unreformed CMEA trade system to structural reform in Hungary. Administrative measures during this period were used to check the influence of CMEA arrangements on financial discipline. Since January 1, 1991, trading with CMEA countries has been at world market prices, with settlement in convertible currencies. This involves a significant terms of trade loss for Hungary and a major loss of revenues for the budget (see Section X). It will entail major economic restructuring, yielding improved economic efficiency over the longer term.

The Exchange Rate System and Export Incentives

The 1968 reform made the exchange rate a potential instrument of economic policy by unifying a multitude of effective exchange rates. These rates had been differentiated, during the period of traditional central planning, virtually by individual products through a system of "price equalization taxes and subsidies." In addition to an "official" exchange rate used for statistical purposes with no operational significance, the new exchange rate system included (through 1976) a commercial rate—called the "foreign trade multiplier," originally set to equal the average cost in forints of earning a unit of foreign exchange in nonruble exports—and a noncommercial rate, called the "tourist rate." The official rate was abolished in 1976 and the noncommercial rate—set at Ft 30 per U.S. dollar in 1968, as against a commercial rate of Ft 60 per U.S. dollar, to reflect the heavy subsidization of consumer goods and services purchased by foreign travelers in Hungary—was gradually moved closer to the commercial rate beginning in 1979 and merged with the latter in October 1981. Separate exchange rates applied vis-à-vis the transferable ruble—originally set in 1968 at Ft 40 per TR—for the settlement of trade with other members of the CMEA. Bilateral exchange rates vis-à-vis the national currencies of CMEA countries were established for noncommercial transactions based on the hypothetical consumption basket of a diplomatic family.

After unifying the commercial exchange rate in 1968, exports and imports were valued in domestic currency at foreign currency prices multiplied by this exchange rate and adjusted for customs tariffs, import turnover taxes, and subsidies. Since the introduction of the competitive price system in 1980, a producers' differential turnover tax was imposed on the prices of energy and raw materials imported from the CMEA area to raise them to the level of corresponding domestic prices, which, in turn, were linked to world market prices (see Section IV). Although this tax was levied to correct distortions stemming from CMEA pricing rules, a tax rebate for exporters on the differential producers' turnover tax was in effect from 1980 to 1988 to stimulate exports to the convertible currency area.

Further efforts to promote convertible currency exports included subsidies for agriculture and food processing proportional to the value of the agricultural content of such exports; so-called modernization grants provided to improve international competitiveness; preferential treatment of exporters under various wage regulations; investment incentives based on preferential credits; equity allocations; various forms of tax rebates; and preferential interest rates on the refinancing of export credits. The fees attached to imports—including the licensing fee, statistical fee, and customs clearance fee—were also varied over time for balance of payments reasons.

Limiting the influence of foreign inflation on domestic prices was a main priority in the conduct of exchange rate policy with respect to convertible currencies (Chart 4).[1] Although the official principles of exchange rate policy also included a need to maintain adequate export profitability, the conduct of exchange rate policy was dominated by the perception that devaluations led primarily to a loosening of the financial discipline of exporters and helped only to sustain intramarginal exports without contributing to stronger export competitiveness. The authorities thus avoided currency devaluations aimed at bolstering competitiveness through 1982.[2] Through 1988, the authorities frequently discouraged the full pass-through of the effect of devaluations to domestic prices, in order to strengthen the expenditure-switching effect of devaluation under the competitive price system that relied on export prices to guide domestic prices.

[1] The exchange rate relative to convertible currencies was pegged to a basket of nine currencies, each of which accounted for at least 1 percent of convertible export receipts, weighted with the share of those currencies in Hungary's convertible trade turnover.

[2] A major revaluation vis-à-vis convertible currencies and the transferable ruble took effect on January 1, 1976; at that time, the authorities formally introduced the commercial exchange rate to replace the foreign trade multiplier.

Chart 4. Exchange Rate Developments, January 1980–January 1991
(1980=100)

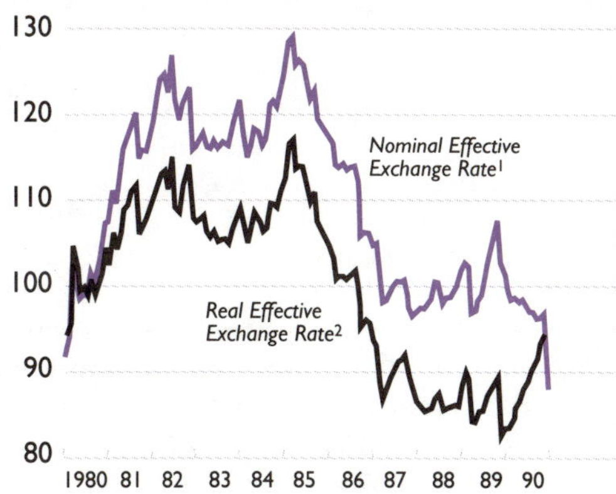

Sources: IMF *International Financial Statistics;* and IMF staff estimates.

[1]Trade-weighted index; based on average monthly exchange rates.

[2]Trade-weighted relative consumer price indices in common currency; based on average monthly exchange rates and prices. For the purpose of calculating the real effective exchange rate, Hungary's price index was reduced by 7.8 percent from January 1988 on, in order to neutralize the effect of the introduction of value-added tax on January 1, 1988.

Even though the authorities increasingly used the exchange rate as an instrument of external adjustment, concerns about the inflationary effect of devaluation continued to constrain exchange rate policy. Nevertheless, in December 1989 and in the first two months of 1990, the forint was depreciated by 15 percent against the basket of convertible currencies (Chart 4). A first step toward introducing a limited foreign exchange market was the Government's authorization, in March 1989, of commercial banks to act as agents for their customers in buying foreign exchange from the NBH (see Section VIII).

Beginning in 1988, every Hungarian citizen was given the right to obtain a passport valid for five years and to travel freely with convertible foreign currency of at least Ft 5,000 (about $100). In 1988, travel allowances were raised to the equivalent of $360 for all adult residents for the period 1988–90, with allowances also available for railway or airline tickets or gasoline. However, faced with substantial travel-related outflows, the authorities in November 1989 reduced these allowances to $50 a person annually, during 1988–91, with bonuses if the allowances were not used until 1990 or 1991. In addition, from December 1989, a VAT of 25 percent was imposed on private imports that were a main source of foreign exchange outflows recorded in the travel account. From September 1989 on, the authorities eased regulations on the declaration requirements for resident foreign currency deposits in Hungarian banks, effectively permitting all residents to hold such deposits. The authorities hoped that such deposits—on which a competitive tax-exempt interest was paid—would constitute an attractive alternative to deposits in foreign banks or cash holdings.

The new Government, faced with large external shocks (see Section X), depreciated the forint by a further 15 percent in January 1991. With the demise of the old CMEA trading arrangements, this rate applies to all trade transactions. With the sharp reduction in trade restrictions in 1991, and the end of the CMEA trading arrangements, the role of exchange rate policy has been considerably enhanced. The Government has announced its intention to achieve convertibility of the forint for current transactions by 1993. It will achieve this objective in a way that does not endanger domestic or external stability. As an intermediate step, the Government intends to create in the second half of 1991 an interbank currency market. With the liberal approval of trade-related foreign exchange transactions, convertibility has already been achieved for most current transactions of the enterprise sector. Given that exchange regulations guarantee the transfer of foreign investors' profits and capital, convertibility for most transactions by foreign investors has also been achieved in 1991.

VI Reform of the Wage System and Labor Market Policy

The wage structure under the system of classical central planning reflected the importance of providing educational and health care services free, housing and communal services at a nominal cost, and other basic consumer goods at heavily subsidized prices. The wage structure was deliberately biased in favor of blue collar workers. The structure of basic wages was laid out in separate matrices of pay scales for blue collar and white collar employees and managerial personnel. Labor income from the socialized sector was subject to no income tax other than a moderate pension contribution by employees. This wage system created a sizable gap between the component of remuneration that represented labor costs for enterprises and the effective disposable income of households; the latter included consumer price subsidies and social benefits in money and kind, financed mainly by heavy taxes on enterprises.

After the 1968 economic reform, wage policy norms were intended to control purchasing power but also to stimulate a more efficient use of labor in an environment of greater enterprise independence. The authorities used various mechanisms to achieve these ends, including heavy taxation of wage increases above a certain level; these taxes were based alternatively on the enterprise wage bill or average wage (providing an allowance for falling employment), with a minimum tax-free wage increase applicable to all enterprises, and performance indicators linking the permissible wage increase to gross value added or profitability. Differential schemes also existed, for periods, for wage increases for enterprises subject to competitive pricing rules, and for agriculture, with wage premia from after-tax profits alternately included and excluded from wage regulation. With the introduction of the personal income tax in 1988, gross wages were increased by an average of 16 percent to compensate for the incidence of the new tax. Wage regulation was intensified to forestall the risk of wage overruns. Penalties on management premia were increased where overruns on the centrally established limits were accommodated, while a more flexible scheme was introduced for certain enterprises (members of a so-called wage club).

A new round of wage reform was introduced at the beginning of 1989. A key innovation was that wages in the competitive sector began to be determined through collective bargaining carried out at the national and enterprise levels. At the central level, the negotiations took place within a new National Interest Coordination Council, composed of representatives of the Government, the Chamber of Commerce and associations of cooperatives, and the national trade union organization. In addition, all wage increases were subject to the 50 percent corporate profit tax, with a tax rebate granted to enterprises whose wage increases were below a certain proportion of the rate of increase of their value added, determined by the National Interest Coordination Council. At the same time, the Government agreed to abstain from any further interference with the freedom of enterprises in the competitive sector to determine individual earnings.

For 1989, the Council approved for wage negotiations at the enterprise level a value of 0.5 for the maximum ratio of the increase of wages to that of value added for an enterprise to qualify for the above tax rebate. In addition, representatives of the employers and of the trade union organization also agreed to recommend in the Council's name a minimum of 3 percent and an upper limit of 10 percent for the increases in the wage bill to be negotiated in individual enterprises. For 1990, increases in the enterprise wage bill that exceeded the increase in value added of the firm were not treated as costs and could not be deducted from the base of the company profit tax. Firms with revenues of less than Ft 20 million were not subject to the regulation, nor were joint ventures with foreign corporations.

The authorities recognized the key importance of wage liberalization in enhancing economic efficiency. They adopted a plethora of wage schemes since 1968, and wage reform became a permanent concern of the economic administration. Although wage regulation schemes largely prevented sizable wage overruns associated with loose financial discipline, they did not help widen the narrow wage dispersion nor correct the distortions in the wage structure. This reflected competing and inconsistent objectives of successive wage reforms, influenced by sociopolitical constraints on the scope of acceptable income differentiation. Unlike the reform of prices, the authorities undertook no systematic realignment of wages aimed at reversing the low labor costs of enterprises coupled with the high taxes on profits to finance consumer price subsidies; neither did they seek to correct the wage and salary bias in favor of blue collar workers introduced earlier. The Government reduced retail price subsidies on several occasions but simultaneously granted partial income compensation, which tended to reinforce the egalitarian structure of wages and salaries. Enterprises were also reluctant to exhaust even the limited scope for differentiation of wages and salaries that would have been allowed by existing wage regulations.

The new Government seeks to make wage growth more responsive to labor market conditions and financial pressures on enterprises, thereby reducing the importance of tax-based incomes policies and central wage agreements. It believes that market-determined wages will promote structural change and efficient resource use. Nevertheless, pending the full imposition of market discipline on state enterprises, for these enterprises the Government has continued to use tax-based wage regulations to reinforce the impact of fiscal and monetary policy restraint on curbing wage growth. For 1991, the Government decided that:

- if the enterprise wage bill does not rise by more than 18 percent, no tax applies;
- if the enterprise wage bill increases by between 18 percent and 28 percent, the increase exceeding 18 percent is subject to the profit tax; and
- if the wage bill rises by more than 28 percent, the entire increase is subject to the profit tax.

In addition, the savings arising from reduced employment may be used tax-free for salary increases up to 5 percent.

Labor Market Policy

Management prerogatives concerning dismissal were limited by a narrow interpretation of the concept of full employment and job security. Whereas enterprises were legally allowed to lay off employees, management had to consult with trade union representatives and give advance notice to the competent local authorities. As managers sought to avoid conflict with the trade union and local authorities, dismissals were rare. The relatively high labor turnover thus resulted from mobility decisions of employees. As a result, the labor market was characterized by underemployment combined with labor shortages in many enterprises.

In 1983, the authorities relaxed the requirement for managers to secure new jobs for employees prior to dismissal, created a legal framework for temporary financial support for and retraining of dismissed persons, and began to set up a network of labor exchanges. A new scheme to assist dismissed workers, introduced in 1986, specified a minimum three months' notice during which the labor exchange was obliged to find the dismissed worker a new job. If the exchange could not provide new employment requiring the same training and no more than one hour's commuting time and paying no less than 90 percent of the initial salary, the dismissed person qualified for a transfer payment ranging from full compensation to 60 percent of his initial salary on a declining scale over a nine-month period. In 1987, an Employment Policy Fund was instituted to finance the above relocation transfers, job retraining, and new job-creation facilities.

In 1988, the Government extended nationwide a scheme of interest-free credits—which had been applied in 1988 in selected regions—to stimulate the creation of independent enterprises by qualified persons laid off during restructurings. Furthermore, the authorities upgraded job retraining facilities and took steps to establish unemployment benefits for those who qualified; the eligibility criteria were strict and included collaboration with the labor exchanges in search of new employment. A Professional Training Fund was also established in 1989 to promote the employment of newly qualified graduates. To finance these schemes, budget appropriations for the Employment Policy Fund were doubled to Ft 2.4 billion in 1989 and to Ft 5.5 billion in 1990. Not all of the new schemes were successful: the program granting interest-free credits for self employment was widely abused and was terminated in 1990. A major constraint on labor mobility was the difficulty of transfers in light of the highly segmented housing market.

The new Government's approach, as noted above, is to rely on a market-based wage determination, while assisting the unemployed. The Government has taken several measures to improve the operation of the labor market and to enhance the skills of the work force. A National Training Council was established in early 1991 to improve regional adult training programs. The Government plans to establish regional labor centers and labor exchanges and to improve vocational training. It also intends to enhance labor mobility by tackling rigidities in the provision of housing. Recent measures to overhaul the subsidization of private and public housing, and the restructuring of the construction sector, represent initial steps toward a more efficient use of housing resources (see Section VIII). To satisfy better the growing need for unemployment compensation, the authorities established in 1991 an unemployment insurance scheme (Solidarity Fund), partly financed by employer and employee contributions. Measures to promote small- and medium-sized enterprises are also expected to reduce unemployment. The Government is developing a social assistance program to improve the targeting of social assistance benefits and establish a cost-sharing arrangement between the State and local governments. It is determined to provide a social safety net for the poor, the elderly, children, and the disabled.

VII Fiscal Reform

When the central Government lost the authority to issue plan directives to enterprises as part of the 1968 economic reform, it resorted to a complex system of taxes and subsidies attached to factors of production, products, and incomes as a key instrument of economic policy. The primary tasks of the tax regime were to (i) secure revenues to finance government operations, a large part of investment, and sizable collective consumption expenditures; and (ii) redistribute current enterprise profits and retained earnings in pursuit of production, trade, income, and price policy objectives.

The system grew more complex during the 1970s, particularly because of the introduction of various tax preferences, new production taxes—designed to withdraw windfall gains from enterprises benefiting from external factors, including foreign price developments and certain "economic regulators"—and a new profit tax. Many of the changes were adopted in conjunction with policies aimed at insulating the domestic economy from a full pass-through of world market price developments during this period. The fiscal measures were strongly differentiated by branch; for some enterprises, they were individually negotiated with the authorities, with the concessions generally favoring large and relatively inefficient companies. The result was a system of multiple taxation with multiple aims that tended to violate the basic intent of the 1968 reform and the general principles of neutrality, transparency, stability, and equity of taxation.

The authorities acted to simplify the tax system with the price reform of 1980; the reform also shifted the burden of taxation from the factors of production to profits and incomes. Part of the gain in the transparency and predictability of fiscal instruments was subsequently eroded, however, by frequent tax adjustments and confiscatory withdrawals of enterprise financial assets, notably, the confiscation in 1982–84 of retained earnings of enterprises accumulated in so-called reserve funds and development funds. These revenues were allocated to a State Lending Fund of the budget and to an Intervention Fund created in 1984 to provide extrabudgetary support for crisis industries or areas in economic decline.

The 1980 reform was reversed in 1985 with a shift in the burden of taxation from profits and retained earnings back to the factors of production (Table 1). The authorities ended confiscatory intervention, along with the segmentation of retained earnings of enterprises in separate funds earmarked for different purposes. They abolished a 40 percent levy on enterprise depreciation allowances and introduced a new tax of 10 percent on the wage bill of enterprises—with preferential rates and complete exemptions for several branches—payable from after-tax profits; a new tax of 3 percent on the net worth of enterprises—with several branches exempt; and a new conjunctural investment tax with a general rate of 18 percent—with certain branches exempt and others subject to penalty rates.

The 1988–90 Tax Reforms

At the beginning of 1988, the authorities introduced a VAT and a personal income tax (PIT). A year later they unveiled a new enterprise profit tax (EPT) and abolished several existing direct and indirect taxes. The reform was aimed at correcting the distortions stemming from a discretionary and selective system of taxation. The excessive burden of direct taxes on enterprises was to be reduced—offset in part by the grossing up of wages paid in the socialized sector by the equivalent of the personal income tax liability of wage earners—and an increasing share of budget revenue was to be obtained from taxes on personal incomes and final consumption.

The introduction of the VAT and PIT in 1988 was accompanied by the elimination of most consumer turnover taxes,[3] the net worth tax, the investment tax, the municipal contribution from profits, and the wage bill tax on enterprises.

[3] Although these were simplified in 1985, approximately one hundred rates remained in effect.

Table 1. Consolidated Budget[1,2,3]

	1984	1985	1986	1987	1988	1989	Prov. 1990
				(Billions of forint)			
Revenues	566.9	588.4	571.1	615.7	706.3	836.8	990.6
Wage tax and other social security contributions[4]	119.4	145.8	148.4	157.5	194.9	320.0	407.8
Profit taxes	142.9	137.7	134.1	149.4	137.6	134.0	163.6
Production and capital taxes	25.4	41.9	44.5	33.0	8.4	1.8	—
Indirect taxes	193.6	197.3	197.0	221.4	343.5	347.6	388.2
Turnover taxes	(169.1)	(169.7)	(164.3)	(186.7)	(307.2)	(298.6)	(335.2)
Tariffs	(24.5)	(27.6)	(32.7)	(34.7)	(36.3)	(48.9)	(53.0)
Other revenues	85.6	65.7	47.1	54.4	21.9	33.5	31.0
Expenditures	544.1	598.5	605.6	651.1	718.3	851.2	979.2
Capital expenditures	58.9	61.8	40.5	43.5	47.6	37.5	29.0
Subsidies	154.5	160.2	172.6	177.1	166.4	186.9[5]	182.3
Of which:							
Housing loan subsidies	(7.7)	(7.4)	(8.6)	(10.0)	(25.9)	(69.8)[5]	(72.7)
Social security[4]	120.0	131.5	142.1	154.7	216.6	272.3	359.3
Goods and services	183.7	206.9	186.2	201.7	207.9	257.3	303.8
Other	27.1	38.1	64.2	74.1	79.8	97.1	104.8
Of which:							
Interest payments	(. . .)	(. . .)	(. . .)	(32.5)	(41.0)	(41.3)	(60.0)
Overall balance (*GFS* basis)	22.8	–10.1	–34.5	–35.4	–12.0	–14.3	11.5[6]
(In percent of GDP)	(2.3)	(–1.0)	(–3.2)	(–2.9)	(–0.9)	(–0.8)	(0.6)[6]
Financing, net (*GFS* basis)	–22.8	10.1	34.5	35.4	12.0	14.3	–11.5
Bank financing, net	–17.8	6.2	33.5[7]	46.7	3.5	44.1	–13.9
Other domestic financing, net	–6.3	3.7	9.6	–3.7	16.9	–19.4	–12.2
External financing, net	1.3	0.2	–8.6	–7.6	–8.4	–10.3	–9.8
Memorandum items							
Overall balance							
(Hungarian presentation)	–3.7	–15.7	–46.9	–34.8	–19.7	–51.8	–5.5
(In percent of GDP)	(–0.4)	(–1.5)	(–4.3)	(–2.8)	(–1.4)	(–3.0)	(–0.3)
Reconciliation between *GFS* and Hungarian presentation	–26.5	–5.6	–12.4	0.6	–7.7	–37.4	–17.0
Amortization of domestic debt	(–10.0)	(–3.8)	(–3.8)	(–4.4)	(–6.7)	(–7.2)	(–7.2)
Net external financing	(1.3)	(0.2)	(–8.6)	(–7.6)	(–8.4)	(–10.3)	(–9.8)
Timing differences, other	(–17.8)	(–2.0)	(—)	(12.6)	(7.4)	(–19.9)	(—)

Sources: Ministry of Finance; and IMF estimates.

[1]Consolidated with social security and housing funds, but excludes extrabudgetary funds, and, since 1986, local authorities.

[2]Starting in 1987, CMEA equalization payments are on a net basis.

[3]The *Government Finance Statistics* balance reclassifies to 1988 Ft 6.9 billion on interest subsidies included in the 1989 balance in the official presentation. In addition, carryovers of interest expenditures in the official presentation of Ft 12.6 billion in 1988 and Ft 13.1 billion in 1989 have been reclassified to the preceding year.

[4]Starting in 1989, includes increased transfers to the Social Security Fund from budgetary institutions and local authorities following the unification of contribution rates.

[5]Includes Ft 12.2 billion, reclassified from capital expenditures. Programmed and actual expenditures for 1990 were prepared on the same basis.

[6]Would total –Ft 8.0 billion (–0.4 percent of GDP) if the State Development Institution were included. This is the basis on which the 1991 budget has been prepared.

[7]Excludes borrowing to finance the acquisition of bank shares.

The VAT applied to most goods and services, with special provisions for small firms, household services, and housing construction. The tax was fully rebated on exports; no rebate was granted in 1988 on socialized sector investment expenditures, but the rebate was phased in gradually beginning in 1989, reaching 60 percent in 1990. In 1990, investment in disadvantaged areas, or for environmental protection or by joint ventures, had a zero VAT rate. The VAT rates ranged from the normal 25 percent, to a reduced rate of 15 percent mostly for services, and to full exemption for more than

40 percent of consumer expenditures, mainly food, household fuel, and transportation and communication services.

The PIT applied to the global income of individuals. It taxed for the first time wages earned in the socialized sector and superseded the schedular income taxes paid on various private economic activities. Socialized sector wages were grossed up to preserve the net income of employees. Secondary incomes from private activities were aggregated and taxed at the marginal rate, which increased the tax burden on such activities.

Originally, the PIT rates ranged from 20 percent to 60 percent in eleven brackets, with an average tax rate of 14.5 percent. Of five million potential taxpayers, about 20 percent were expected to fall below the threshold of a general tax-free allowance of Ft 48,000 a year—equivalent to about two thirds average earnings in the socialized sector. The taxable unit was the individual rather than the family, but a separate standard deduction was granted for the cost of raising children. Special provisions applied to incomes from small-scale farming and from intellectual activities, and most social benefits were exempt, with a tax-free allowance available for pensions. Interest and dividend incomes were subject to a separate flat rate tax of 20 percent, and generous provisions were granted for the deductibility of savings for housing purposes and interest on housing loans. For incomes from employment and interest, the tax was withheld at source. In 1989, the tax-free allowance was raised to Ft 55,000 a year and the marginal tax rates were lowered to between 17 percent and 56 percent, the number of brackets to eight, and the average tax rate to about 14.6 percent. In 1990, the number of brackets was reduced to five and the top marginal rate to 50 percent. Higher-than-expected wage increases, however, placed individuals in higher marginal tax brackets, thereby raising the average tax rate to an estimated 16.4 percent.

The EPT introduced in 1989 was aimed at providing a uniform system of taxation for all enterprises. Accordingly, the "countervalue tax" on subcontracting to economic partnerships of employees was abolished and the entrepreneurial tax integrated into the EPT. Individual undertakings, including small-scale farming, remained subject only to the PIT but could have their profits taxed under the EPT. In a further effort to streamline the tax system, the authorities removed several production taxes in metallurgy, the chemical industry, transportation, and public services. An EPT rate of 50 percent was approved with a 4 percent surcharge; a reduced 40 percent rate applied to the first Ft 3 million tranche of the annual profit of any enterprise, in order to favor small businesses. Under the EPT, several tax preferences were maintained, with a view to stimulating such economic activities as farming, food processing, and grocery trade, as well as research and development, cultural, health, and social services. In 1990, the EPT rate was reduced to 40 percent (35 percent for the first Ft 3 million of profits); an 18 percent dividend was introduced, payable by state enterprises on their after-tax profits—a measure intended to equalize the treatment of all enterprises with respect to taxation and the return on capital to owners.

Tax incentives were also given to joint ventures with foreign partners. Tax allowances of 20 percent on the payable EPT were granted to joint ventures with a foreign share of at least 20 percent, or Ft 5 million. The allowance could rise to 100 percent for activities in priority sectors during the first five years, to be lowered to 60 percent in the sixth year. Profit taxes on reinvested earnings of the foreign partner were fully refunded. Effective January 1, 1989, a new Foreign Investment Law included guarantees for the protection of the investment and the transfer of profits and all other stipulations governing foreign investment in Hungary.

The tax reforms of 1988–90 sought to establish a more transparent, neutral, and stable financial environment for economic decision making by both households and enterprises. The rules of taxation were to be subject to parliamentary approval and major steps were taken to streamline the structure of the tax system. However, distortions remained. Under the EPT, not only were many old allowances permitted to continue, but new allowances were introduced in 1989 and 1990. As a result, the marginal effective tax rate on investments varied widely. The standard VAT rate of 25 percent was high because a zero VAT rate applied to many consumer necessities, which created inefficiencies in consumption choice. The PIT applied mostly to cash payments, excluding benefits provided to employees in kind.

In July 1990, the new Government, as part of its corrective fiscal package, increased the dividend payable by state enterprises to 25 percent. In 1991, a major structural change associated with the conversion of CMEA trade to world prices was the elimination of revenues from the differential producer turnover tax on CMEA trade. This revenue loss was partly offset by higher duties on petroleum and luxury products.

The Government recognizes the need for further reform of the tax system. Its objective is to broaden the tax base and lower the burden of direct taxes. For the personal income tax, elimination of current widespread exemptions will permit the introduction of a more gradual progressive scale of taxation, which will provide enhanced incentives. The

Government is considering narrowing the range of VAT rates. It is currently preparing proposals for reform of the tax system. A significant reduction in government spending will permit a lowering of tax revenues relative to GDP, while achieving fiscal balance by 1993.

Budgetary and Social Security Reform

At the time of the adoption of the PIT and VAT in the fall of 1987, Parliament instructed the Government to design a blueprint for comprehensive budgetary reform. The principal aim was to scale down substantially and rationalize government intervention in the economy. The authorities made some progress in this direction; producer and consumer subsidies declined to 13 percent of GDP in 1989, from 21 percent in 1986. In 1989, the National Savings Bank stopped granting exceptionally low-interest housing loans and losses of the newly established Housing Fund's portfolio of low-yielding assets were to be absorbed by the budget (see Section VIII). Housing loans continued to be extended, however, at below-market interest rates. In 1990, the Government took a first step toward reducing the burden of housing finance on the budget by imposing a tax on pre-1989 subsidized housing loans granted at preferential interest rates ranging from zero to 3.5 percent. Rents on local council apartments were also raised by 35 percent. The tax on old housing loans, however, was ruled unconstitutional by the Constitutional Court in March 1990.

The budget reform aimed at replacing broad objectives guiding the provision of health, cultural, social, and housing services to the population—which in many cases remained unfulfilled—by more narrowly but clearly defined services in these areas. Eligibility for these services was, where appropriate, to be more closely related to need. An important element of this program was the reform of social security. A first step in this area was taken at the beginning of 1989, when the authorities separated the social security accounts from the state budget and raised the state sector's employer's contribution to 43 percent, equivalent to the private sector rate. In January 1990, the Social Security Fund assumed responsibility for health care, while in April 1990 responsibility for family allowance transfers was moved from the fund to the state budget. The intention was to adopt guaranteed basic social security entitlements supplemented by insurance-based benefits. Finally, the budget reform also sought to address the issues of revenue sharing with local authorities, funding and control of budgetary institutions, and improvements in the establishment, monitoring, and auditing of budgetary accounts.

Despite the housing finance reforms, the fiscal implications of higher interest rates on the stock of cheap pre-1989 housing loans continued to constrain monetary policy. The overall level of general government expenditures—at more than 60 percent of GDP in 1989—reflected excessive state intervention in the economy and required a heavy tax burden. Social security expenditure (about 17 percent of GDP in 1990), in particular, was poorly targeted, subject to acknowledged abuse, and—given current demographic and economic projections and despite excessively high contribution rates—actuarially unsound.

A radical transformation of public finances is a key element of the Government's strategy to reduce the State's role in the economy. Important steps were taken in the 1991 budget. Subsidies—including consumer, producer, investment, and housing subsidies—are planned to decline to 7 percent of GDP in 1991, from approximately 9 percent in 1990. Interest rates on pre-1989 housing loans have been raised substantially, generating additional payments from each borrower of Ft 1,500 a month, or substantial repayments of old loans with a 50 percent discount. This measure was challenged as unconstitutional on the grounds that it unilaterally changes the terms of old contracts; it was recently ruled constitutional by the Constitutional Court. Investment expenditures by the budget were reduced by about 20 percent. Measures are also planned that will reduce the overall size of public administration, while increasing resources for such essential sectors as tax administration.

The Government is preparing a new Budgetary Framework Law, which is intended to define the functions of central and local governments, establish procedures for expenditure control, and improve fiscal monitoring. The Government's medium-term objective is to reduce substantially state budget spending relative to GDP. This will require an overhaul of the social security system. The Government intends that social systems be supplemented by private insurance, with an important role for nongovernment institutions. It is currently preparing a "white paper" for presentation to Parliament with its proposals for the comprehensive reform of social security programs. Already in 1991, the authorities have acted to increase cost awareness among health consumers and to introduce some reforms of the pension system.

VIII Banking and Capital Market Reform

Although the authorities recognized the need to shift the central guiding force of the financial system from the state budget to a more active credit policy, the New Economic Mechanism blueprint left the banking sector subordinated to financing the national economic plan. The authorities did not significantly alter the highly concentrated and specialized banking system and segmented financial structure of the economy—established in the late 1940s—until the mid-1980s.

The banking sector continued after 1968 to be dominated by the NBH. The NBH performed central banking functions; regulated foreign exchange transactions, with responsibility for conducting almost all external credit operations with the convertible currency area; and, through its credit department and branch offices, acted as the principal banker of the enterprise sector and helped administer government programs in industrial policy and other areas. The volume and allocation of credit by the banking system for investment and working capital purposes was determined by the credit policy guidelines of the NBH, which were approved by the Government in coordination with the national economic plan. The NBH exercised direct control over the allocation of credit, a substantial part of which was funded by foreign borrowing. Interest rates had a small allocative role, and indirect monetary policy instruments were absent.

The other banks in the system continued to be restricted to specialized activities. The State Development Bank's principal task was to prepare, monitor, and finance state investment projects and allocate equity to enterprises; projects were funded by refinancing credits from the NBH, budget transfers, project loans from the International Investment Bank of the CMEA, and enterprises' contributions to project financing. The Hungarian Foreign Trade Bank specialized in foreign currency trade financing of enterprises; it funded itself in the international markets under the supervision of the NBH. The National Savings Bank, supplemented by the Postal Savings network and savings cooperatives, acted as the banker of the general population, private concerns, and local authorities. It collected deposits at low interest rates, most of which were relent at even lower rates for housing. Other banking and financial institutions (including the Central European International Bank, Ltd., established in 1979 as an "offshore" bank in a joint venture between the NBH and six foreign banks) played a peripheral role, mainly conducting foreign exchange and real estate transactions. In addition, beginning in 1983, the authorities set up small experimental financial institutions in the form of specialized funds mainly to finance research and development and venture capital for risky projects.

With the institutional structure of the banking sector remaining essentially unchanged, the segmented pattern of financial flows—in particular the separation of household monetary and credit flows from those of the enterprise sector—was preserved. Although a high proportion of national income was allocated to investment by international standards—with the share of gross capital formation to GDP in the range of 30–35 percent in the 1970s and 25–30 percent in the first half of the 1980s—financial intermediation outside the budget remained limited. In the mid-1980s, about three quarters of investment approved by the State was financed by the budget and enterprise contributions, and the same proportion of enterprise investment was financed by internally generated funds. Enterprise investment was financed this way partly because of a bias of enterprise management in favor of fixed asset formation as against financial savings, which was reinforced by repeated confiscations of accumulated financial assets of profitable enterprises, low interest rates, and a scarcity of savings instruments. For the household sector, in addition to currency holdings and bank deposits, available savings instruments were limited to life insurance policies with the State Insurance Company, small amounts of bonds issued since 1983, cooperative share certificates, and real estate. The financial saving propensity of the population was generally low because precautionary saving was discouraged in light of virtually guaranteed lifetime employment, negative real interest rates on savings deposits, and the availability of heavily subsidized housing loans. Real estate was the principal investment outlet for household savings.

The Government also exerted strong influence over investment by disbursing state loans to finance state-initiated projects, and by having branch ministries participate in vetting credit applications from enterprises and in granting selective credit preferences. The latter included preferential credits under a facility inaugurated in 1976 providing longer-than-usual maturities and interest rebates from the budget to finance eligible projects aimed at export promotion, import substitution, energy conservation, raw materials recycling, and (since 1982) to finance projects sponsored by the International Bank for Reconstruction and Development (IBRD). As a result, access to credit for entirely enterprise-initiated projects was limited, which curtailed the expansion of small profitable enterprises in the socialized and private sectors.

Monetary policy accommodated the inflation rates projected under the annual macroeconomic plans, but over most of the period it avoided adding significantly to inflationary pressures. Credit restrictions were applied periodically, mainly to control expansionary investment cycles; liquidity in the enterprise sector was squeezed by tightening credit ceilings, forcing early repayment of outstanding credits, and, at times, confiscating financial assets. These restrictions were imposed mainly on successful companies. Inefficient enterprises—generally conglomerates in dominant positions vis-à-vis suppliers and customers—accumulated payments arrears and were eventually given access to budgetary support, equity allocations, and bank credit. The latter policy, including the nearly automatic provision of working capital credit to guarantee enterprises' wage payments—which accommodated overstaffing and excessive wage awards—hindered the closure or restructuring of loss-making enterprises and led the NBH and the State Development Bank to acquire a large share of dubious claims on the enterprise sector. Part of such claims was intermittently converted into equity allocations to weak companies.

Reform of the Banking System Since 1985

By the early 1980s, the authorities acknowledged that the existing financial institutions and instruments had blocked their pursuit of both short-term demand management objectives and efficiency gains from long-term structural reforms. They adopted preliminary institutional reforms in 1985; these included separating central banking and commercial banking functions within the NBH, converting the Budapest branch of the NBH into an independent subsidiary, and registering as independent specialized financial institutions several funds earlier established. Various administrative constraints on the flexibility of banking activities were removed: state enterprises were allowed greater freedom to place their time deposits, but not their current account deposits, with the banking institution of their choice; savings cooperatives were authorized to provide similar banking services as the National Savings Bank; and small socialist and private enterprises were permitted to transfer their accounts from the latter bank to both savings cooperatives and the NBH, a move designed to facilitate their transactions with the state enterprise sector. In 1986, a new commercial bank, Citibank Budapest, was established under the joint ownership of Citibank (80 percent) and the NBH (20 percent), authorized in principle to offer all types of banking services to enterprises. Whereas other interest rates continued to be determined administratively, from 1986 on, lending institutions became free to set loan rates to enterprises subject to the constraint that the average rate charged not exceed the refinancing rate of the NBH by more than 1.5 percentage points.

The principal phase of the banking reform, consisting of the establishment of a two-tier banking system, was implemented in January 1987. The domestic commercial banking operations of the NBH and the State Development Bank were taken over by three new commercial banks. The new banks were set up as joint stock companies owned directly by the State and state enterprises. They assumed the deposits and the loan portfolios of their predecessors, with certain banks inheriting a disproportionate share of credits to less creditworthy enterprises and loans at concessional interest rates. Two other banking institutions, including the Foreign Trade Bank, were also authorized to function as full service commercial banks from this date, and new banks, including some with foreign participation, later acceded to the system. In 1987, the authorities lifted the requirement for enterprises to keep their current accounts with a particular commercial bank and authorized the banks to use interest rates to compete for enterprise deposits and loans.

The segmentation between banking services for enterprises and the traditional network of savings institutions for households continued to prevail, however, through 1988. A necessary condition for the integration of banking services between the enterprise and household sectors was reform of the housing finance system, which was introduced on January 1, 1989. The implicit taxation of depositors at the savings institutions as a source of the subsidization of housing loans had already been reduced notably from late 1987 through increases in interest rates on savings deposits. In early 1989, the Government discontinued granting very-low-interest housing loans by the National Savings Bank and transferred the cost of the remaining subsidy elements of new housing credits to the budget. The sizable outstanding stock of concessional loans of the National Savings Bank was transferred to a newly established housing fund in exchange for bonds with market-related yields. The losses of the housing fund from the assumption of the portfolio of low-interest housing loans were covered by budgetary transfers.

These reforms helped free the commercial banks and the savings institutions to compete for the deposit and credit business of customers across the economy. Until the beginning of 1990, strict reserve requirements were imposed on household deposits at commercial banks in order to protect the savings institutions from a drain of funds. Ceilings also remained in place on interest rates on household deposits, although these were generally set high enough to allow positive pre-tax real rates of interest; increasingly, these ceilings were adjusted in line with movements in market rates of interest.

With respect to foreign exchange transactions, banks were authorized to provide foreign-exchange-related services to households beginning in the second half of 1988; from the beginning of 1989, banks could act as agents in foreign exchange purchases of enterprises from the NBH and be involved in forward exchange operations. From September 1989 on, banks were effectively free to take foreign currency deposits of residents. As a further step toward decentralizing foreign exchange operations, certain commercial banks were permitted, beginning in early 1990, to carry out trade-related foreign exchange operations directly with their customers and to maintain correspondent banking relationships with some major international banks. Banks were also permitted to make foreign currency loans for export pre-financing for certain export-related investments.

Along with the institutional reform of the banking sector, the authorities established a system of prudential regulations and banking supervision; at the same time, monetary control shifted gradually from reliance on credit ceilings to indirect instruments affecting the cost of credit. A system of reserve requirements introduced in early 1987 served largely prudential purposes. However, central bank refinancing quotas—including rediscounting of commercial bills—and interest rate policy became the principal instruments of monetary control.

Chart 5. Interest Rates, January 1985–December 1990
(Percent)

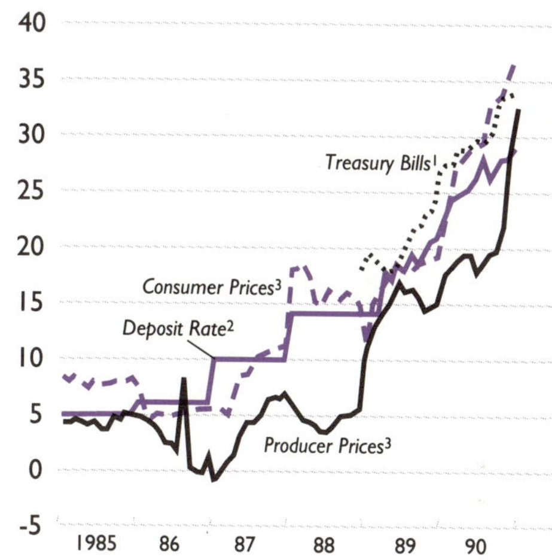

Source: IMF, *International Financial Statistics.*
[1]Treasury bills of 90-day maturity; sold by auction from December 1988.
[2]Two-year time deposit rate.
[3]Twelve monthly percentage change.

Monetary policy instruments were streamlined and rendered more flexible beginning in 1989. A uniform rate was introduced for standard reserve requirements, and interest payments on reserve deposits were discontinued. The role of the rediscount facility and liquidity credits was enhanced and rendered more flexible. The auctioning of treasury bills by the NBH, beginning in December 1988, facilitated a more flexible interest rate policy.

While quantitative refinancing quotas remained proportional to a bank's equity capital and reserves, interest rates on refinancing were raised substantially in December 1989—by 3 percentage points—to 17 percent for the basic refinancing rate and 21 percent for the more widely used "liquidity rate." Subsequently, these rates were adjusted in the light of developments in market-based interest rates (Chart 5).

The new Government will rely more heavily on market-based instruments of monetary and credit control. From the beginning of 1991, all short-term refinancing loans by the NBH have been at market interest rates, with some of these funds made available through auctions. In January 1991, the authorities abolished ceilings on interest rates on household deposits of more than six months' maturity. A new Central Bank Law is being prepared; it will establish the autonomy of the NBH and define the primary responsibility of the NBH as preserving the value of the forint.

The Government recognizes that an efficient financial system is necessary to promote the effective mobilization and reallocation of resources toward their most efficient use. It has therefore taken steps to increase competition in the provision of banking services. In October 1990, the authorities granted general banking licenses to two foreign banks, authorizing them to provide retail banking services. A new Banking Law is being drawn up to introduce internationally accepted prudential regulation, including levels of capital adequacy and the treatment of bad loans.

Other Developments in the Financial System

After a hiatus of thirty years, the authorities resumed issuing bonds in 1981. Initially, local councils issued bonds to finance infrastructural projects, and since 1983 state enterprises have also issued bonds. Bonds were initially placed with enterprises, but sales to households have been permitted since 1984, provided the issue is backed by a state guarantee. The State Development Bank initiated secondary trading of bonds in 1984, and the Budapest Bank assumed the role of residual buyer and seller after adoption of the two-tier banking system in 1987. Activity in the nascent primary and secondary markets flagged after the authorities ceased issuing government guarantees for bonds in early 1987. Bonds also became less attractive as the main underwriters refrained from adjusting bond prices despite the rapid rise in interest rates and increasing competition from treasury bills and certificates of deposit. Further new developments in the securities market included an increase in 1988 in the number of enterprises selling shares, and the opening in early 1988 of the first brokerage house. In 1990, a Securities Market Law was adopted that established a State Securities Supervision Board to regulate the public issuance of securities and the rights and obligations of security traders. Following this, the Budapest Stock Exchange formally reopened operations in June 1990.

Although commercial bills could be issued on the basis of legislation originating in 1877 and a decree from 1965, they remained absent from the financial system from the inception of central planning through the mid-1980s because of a general prohibition of interenterprise financial operations. Financial legislation adopted in 1985 created a new basis for issuing and trading bills. The role of bills remained negligible, however, until 1987, when their discounting at the banks—and their rediscounting with the NBH—increased their importance as an instrument of working capital finance for enterprises.

The state insurance monopoly created by the nationalization of insurance companies in 1949 was abolished in July 1986 and succeeded by two major institutions offering a broader selection of policies. These companies have recently begun to act as institutional investors, investing in the bond market, in bank shares, in real estate, and in treasury bills.

The Government wishes to encourage citizen shareholding as a way of promoting the efficient allocation of capital. It recognizes that a genuine market economy cannot come about without the earliest possible development of the infrastructure of financial information and services. Although the volume of transactions on the Budapest Stock Exchange has been light so far, its growth should be aided by the expansion of private property and privatization. The implementation of laws setting international standards in accounting and auditing planned for 1992 should also promote the exchange's expansion. The Government plans to introduce an Insurance Act in 1991 that will foster the development of the insurance sector to cover the growing economic risks.

IX Agricultural Reform

Agricultural policy in the early 1950s concentrated on extracting resources from the farm sector to underpin a rapid expansion of industry. After two major drives to establish agricultural cooperatives in the early 1950s and during 1959–61, more than two thirds of arable land was shifted from private hands to cooperatives, and the share of socialist ownership—by state farms and cooperatives—rose to 99 percent. This agricultural policy led to a stagnation of output and a major exodus of labor from farming in the first half of the 1950s.

The authorities decided to overhaul farm policy in 1957. They replaced compulsory delivery of products to state procurement agencies at low prices with contracts; they also introduced greater flexibility in marketing agricultural products. About 80 percent of products were delivered to the procurement agencies on a contract basis and some 20 percent traded directly in the market. In 1966, the Government abolished mandatory plan directives regarding production for agricultural cooperatives and in 1968 for state farms, but it continued to intervene informally. Nevertheless, farm prices were kept low relative to industrial prices, given the priority accorded to low food prices. Together with an incomes policy objective of maintaining a rough parity of incomes between agriculture and industry, the operating surplus of farms relative to industrial enterprises was compressed. The profitability of the two sectors was roughly equalized, through fiscal policy, at about one third of value added. Budgetary assistance to the agricultural sector included subsidies for various forms of investment, energy use, and other farm inputs; for the promotion of exports; and for farms operating at higher costs and lower yields than average, owing mainly to poor soil conditions or insufficient mechanization. Whereas agriculture was subject to the same taxes as industry, rates for farms were generally lower.

The notable improvement in Hungary's agricultural performance in the 1970s was attributable largely to greater managerial freedom accorded to state farms and cooperatives, and to a new pragmatic attitude toward small-scale farming operations on household plots and auxiliary farms of the population. Advanced farming technologies were introduced from abroad; these technologies resulted from initiatives of farm managers that introduced agro-industrial activities and joint ventures between state and cooperative farms. Greater managerial freedom and initiative also led agricultural enterprises to compete in nonagricultural activities with enterprises in other branches. This led to the rapid growth of ancillary industrial, construction, and service activities—particularly by cooperative farms—whose share rose to 31 percent of gross farm output in 1987 from 3.5 percent in the 1960s.

The transformation in farming was most pronounced in the privately operated household plots of cooperative members and auxiliary farms of employees of other sectors. The legal limits on the size of household plots were maintained, but restrictions on keeping animals and owning machinery were lifted. The initially hostile attitude of the agricultural administration and cooperatives toward household farming turned favorable, and a pragmatic division of labor and coordination of activities evolved between cooperatives and individuals operating household plots. Farming (on 11 percent of Hungary's arable land) by small producers on private farms, household plots, and auxiliary farms accounted for one third of gross agricultural output in 1987.

Gross agricultural output grew at an annual rate of 3.2 percent from 1970 through 1983. Output stagnated in the subsequent period, however, only partly because of bad weather, and the authorities initiated a review of medium-term agricultural priorities and strategies. They concluded that farming needed structural renewal, based on a reinvigoration of market forces to guide managerial decisions. They took steps to widen the scope of free producer and consumer prices for farm and food products, particularly in early 1990 when most food prices were freed from controls.

The new Government took further steps to liberalize consumer and producer prices for agricultural products at the beginning of 1991 (see Section IV). The objective of its land reform is to link ownership with agricultural production. New legislation seeks to regulate cooperatives, and private land ownership will be promoted.

X Recent Developments and Outlook

During the 1970s, macroeconomic policies in Hungary were sufficiently balanced to prevent chronic shortages and inflationary pressures in consumer markets. Partly because of a delayed response to sharp increases in world prices for oil and other imported raw materials, however, Hungary's convertible currency trade deficit widened steadily in the 1970s, resulting in the buildup of substantial external debt. From the late 1970s to the mid- to late 1980s, the stance of economic policies was reversed frequently, shifting between expansion and restraint, in an attempt to narrow the external imbalance (Table 2).

Against this background, the Government adopted in mid-1987 a medium-term program of economic stabilization and structural reform to address the weak supply performance of the economy, which persisted despite relatively high investment. Pending the benefits of comprehensive structural reform, a substantial share of the initial adjustment was borne by demand restraint—mainly through a reduction in the budget deficit and curtailment of excess liquidity. This resulted in sluggish GDP growth of 1/2 of 1 percent in 1988 and in a 2 percent fall in domestic demand—the largest decline recorded in the 1980s (Table 3). Consumer price inflation rose to 15 percent, mainly because of the introduction of a VAT tax on January 1, 1988. The convertible current account deficit—which reached 6.3 percent of GDP in 1986—narrowed gradually to 2.9 percent in 1988, despite a substantial increase in travel expenditures as Hungarian residents took advantage of relaxed travel and foreign exchange regulations. The external adjustment slowed the previously rapid growth of external convertible debt.

The adjustment program faltered in 1989. Real output declined for the first time since 1985, and consumer price inflation increased to 19 percent. The rise in inflation reflected, in part, accommodating financial policies. Wages also increased faster than planned, particularly in the early part of the year; the rapid pace of wage increase was the result of large wage awards granted by enterprises enjoying greater freedom over wage determination and high liquidity, owing to a much weaker than planned fiscal policy and a large ruble trade surplus.

The loose financial policies led to a widening of the convertible current account deficit to $1.4 billion in 1989 (5 percent of GDP), compared with $0.8 billion in the previous year. A small improvement in the trade balance, reflecting improved terms of trade, was more than offset by a large deterioration in the services account. The latter was due primarily to large travel outflows, encouraged by an unduly favorable regime for personal imports and by an overvalued currency. It also reflected larger debt service payments and—increasingly during the course of the year—capital flight.

In response to the resulting convertible currency drain, the Hungarian authorities adopted policies in late 1989 to achieve domestic and external adjustment and to preserve Hungary's external solvency. A stand-by arrangement with the IMF was concluded in March 1990 for approximately $200 million, equivalent to 30 percent of Hungary's quota in the IMF. This arrangement sought to reduce the convertible current account deficit to $550 million in 1990, and to reduce the current account surplus in nonconvertible currencies to $35 million in 1990 from $800 million in 1989. It also sought to contain domestic inflation to about 20 percent and to sustain economic reform. In pursuit of these goals, the Hungarian authorities:

- tightened fiscal policy—including lending by the State Development Institution—by roughly 2 percentage points of GDP relative to 1989;
- limited the expansion of domestic credit to well below the rate of inflation;
- increased domestic interest rates;
- depreciated the forint against convertible currencies by 15 percent and tightened household access to foreign currency; and
- lowered ruble export quotas while taking administrative measures to ensure adherence to these quotas.

The authorities, as discussed earlier, also adopted various structural reforms. These included

Table 2. Selected Economic and Financial Indicators

	1983	1984	1985	1986	1987	1988	1989	Prov. 1990
	(Annual percent change, unless otherwise specified)							
National income and prices								
GDP at constant prices	0.7	2.7	–0.3	0.7	3.9	–0.2	–0.2	–5.0
Domestic demand at constant prices[1]	–1.7	0.3	0.4	3.2	3.4	–2.7	2.9	–9.7
GDP deflator	5.0	6.3	5.9	4.6	8.5	15.1	22.1	27.0
Consumer prices[2]	7.3	8.3	8.1	5.4	10.8	14.7	18.9	33.4
External sector								
Nonruble exports, f.o.b. (in U.S. dollars)	0.3	–1.7	–8.5	0.1	11.6	16.5	5.5	15.5
Nonruble imports, c.i.f. (in U.S. dollars)	–1.3	–3.5	1.3	13.4	9.1	–1.4	5.1	9.9
Nonruble export volume	10.8	4.7	–6.7	–3.9	5.0	8.8	4.8	10.0
Nonruble import volume	6.4	0.4	2.6	0.7	2.6	–6.8	7.0	3.3
Nonruble terms of trade (deterioration –)	–2.4	–2.4	–0.7	–7.5	—	1.1	2.4	–1.4
Nominal effective exchange rate (depreciation –)	–3.9	1.5	4.0	–9.3	–10.8	–1.7	3.2	–3.8
Real effective exchange rate (depreciation –)	–4.7	1.7	3.3	–10.3	–10.1	–4.6	0.9	1.8
Money and credit								
Broad money	3.0	2.7	11.4	9.2	10.2	3.3	13.3	23.8
Domestic credit	3.6	4.8	6.3	12.2	12.4	5.4	5.7	9.6
Velocity (GDP relative to end-year M2)	2.0	2.2	2.1	2.0	2.1	2.3	2.4	2.4
Interest rate (annual rate, two-year time deposit for households)	3.0	3.0	5.0	6.0	10.0	14.0	14.0	24.0
	(Percent of GDP, unless otherwise specified)							
Consolidated budget balance[3]	–1.1	1.4	–1.0	–3.2	–2.9	–0.9	–0.8	0.6
Revenue	60.9	60.8	56.9	52.5	51.4	50.1	49.1	52.1
Expenditure	62.1	59.4	57.9	55.6	54.3	51.0	49.8	51.5
Gross domestic investment[4]	26.5	25.7	25.0	26.9	26.7	25.4	26.4	24.8
Gross domestic savings[1]	28.4	28.9	27.1	25.5	26.2	28.2	26.5	28.5
External current account balance in convertible currencies	0.3	0.3	–4.1	–6.3	–3.4	–2.9	–4.9	0.4
Gross external debt in convertible currencies[5]	54.2	57.5	63.9	71.3	74.1	73.2	75.5	64.6
Debt service ratio in convertible currencies, in percent of merchandise export earnings[6]	48.7	55.0	88.1	99.9	74.2	63.8	55.4	57.0
	(Millions of U.S. dollars, unless otherwise specified)							
External current account balance in convertible currencies	71	65	–846	–1,495	–879	–804	–1,438	127
External current account balance in nonconvertible currencies	–251	–26	390	133	203	232	818	114
Overall balance of payments in convertible currencies	489	317	457	105	–547	175	81	–562

Sources: Hungarian authorities; and IMF staff estimates and projections.
[1]With personal consumption on a "territorial" basis through 1988, and a "national" basis thereafter. Personal consumption on a territorial (national) basis excludes (includes) consumption by Hungarians abroad and includes (excludes) consumption by foreigners in Hungary. Prior to 1989, the difference between consumption measured on, respectively, a territorial and a national basis, was relatively small.
[2]Percent change from the beginning to the end of the year.
[3]Based on the IMF's *Government Finance Statistics*.
[4]Including stockbuilding.
[5]Including the use of IMF resources.
[6]Debt service, including IMF repurchases, in percent of earnings from merchandise exports.

Table 3. Sources and Uses of GDP

	In Billions of Forint, at Current Prices	In Percent of Total	Percent Change at Constant Prices[1]							
	1989	1989	1971–75	1976–80	1981–85	1986	1987	1988	1989	*Prov.* 1990
Sources										
Industry	510.7	34.6	7.3	4.1	2.4	–0.5	3.4	0.1	–3.0	–10.3
Agriculture and forestry	239.1	16.2	3.9	2.2	3.0	3.4	–2.3	8.0	0.1	–8.1
Construction[2]	107.6	7.3	7.4	4.3	–1.3	0.3	5.9	–4.9	–0.4	–1.9
Transportation and communications	122.5	8.3	5.2	2.7	1.6	3.5	5.0	2.0	3.5	1.3
Other material sectors[3]	196.2	13.3	7.6	2.4	2.1	1.4	7.2	–10.1	3.3	–3.6
Nonmaterial services	298.9	20.3	5.7	4.1	3.2	–2.6	8.0	1.8	–2.0	–3.9
Total	1,475.0	100.0	6.2	3.4	2.2	1.3	3.9	0.1	–0.7	–6.2
Customs duties, net turnover taxes, and valuation differences	241.7	. . .	. . .	. . .	. . .	. . .	. . .	. . .	. . .	. . .
GDP	1,716.7	. . .	6.3	3.3	1.8	0.7	3.9	–0.2	–0.2	–5.6[4]
Uses										
Consumption	1,204.9	70.2	4.8	2.9	1.5	2.4	3.3	–2.8	–0.3	–5.4
Personal consumption[5]	(1,018.4)	(59.3)	(4.7)	(2.6)	(1.4)	(2.0)	(3.7)	(–4.2)	(0.4)	(–5.6)
Public consumption	(186.5)	(10.9)	(5.0)	(4.7)	(2.1)	(4.6)	(0.5)	(5.5)	(–4.0)	(–4.3)
Gross fixed investment	345.0	20.1	6.9	2.2	–3.2	2.9	9.1	–9.0	3.6	–4.8
Final domestic demand	1,549.9	90.3	5.4	2.7	0.3	2.5	4.7	–4.4	0.7	–5.2
Stockbuilding[6]	108.7	6.3	. . .	. . .	. . .	0.7	–1.2	1.7	–0.6	–1.4
Domestic demand	1,658.6	96.6	5.7	2.5	0.1	3.2	3.4	–2.7	—	–6.5
Foreign balance[6,7]	58.1	3.4	. . .	. . .	. . .	–2.0	0.4	2.5	–0.2	0.1
GDP[2]	1,716.7	100.0	6.3	3.3	1.8	0.7	3.9	–0.2	–0.2	–5.6[4]

Sources: CSO, *Statistical Yearbook;* IMF, *International Financial Statistics;* Hungarian authorities; and IMF staff estimates.

[1]Annual average percent change at 1976 prices through 1975, at 1981 prices from 1976 through 1985, and at 1986 prices thereafter.

[2]Data at constant prices for 1986 on exclude terms of trade losses on CMEA investment.

[3]Trade, water economy, and other material sectors.

[4]Including unallocated reserve of 0.8 percent of GDP.

[5]Including social benefits in kind and net receipts from tourism.

[6]Percentage contribution to GDP growth.

[7]The foreign balance as a component of GDP does not account for factor payments (including interest) and net travel earnings, which are included in personal consumption.

further price and import liberalization, decentralization of the banking system, and measures to accelerate enterprise restructuring.

The Government that assumed office in May 1990 emphasized its commitment to policies supported by the stand-by arrangement. To this end, the Government adopted in July a fiscal package including reduced subsidies on agricultural exports; higher excise taxes for electricity, gasoline, cigarettes, and liquor; reduced tax allowances; increased dividend payments accruing to the State; and reduced spending in certain areas to meet the fiscal objectives of the program. It also took further measures to raise interest rates (Chart 5). Taking advantage of the better-than-planned performance in the convertible balance of payments in the early part of the year, the Government, in July, announced a lower target deficit of $400 million for 1990.

Implementation of these policies has achieved some important successes. The convertible current account recorded a surplus in 1990 for the first time since 1984. This better-than-planned performance occurred despite disruptions to Soviet oil supplies—which required the substitution of high-priced imports from the West—and the worst drought this century. It resulted from a strong export performance reflecting tight financial policies, which compressed domestic demand. The curbs on ruble exports—which achieved broad balance in ruble trade—ensured that convertible currency export markets were the only source of potential expansion. Exports of small, private firms grew substantially. Travel and transfer receipts were also much stronger than forecast, as Hungary enjoyed a boom in tourism. The convertible current account surplus permitted Hungary to preserve its external solvency, albeit with a low level of reserves. This was possible despite a much weaker capital account than forecast. A shortfall in medium-term borrowing and outflows of short-term capital resulted from spreading concerns about Hungary's creditworthiness. These concerns followed the announcement of a moratorium on principal payments by Bulgaria at the end of March 1990 and payments difficulties in the U.S.S.R., as well as uncertainty surrounding the elections and the new Government's policy toward servicing the debt. The net outflows were partly offset by a doubling of receipts from inward direct foreign investment to $0.4 billion.

Domestically, results were mixed. Output is estimated to have declined by up to 6 percent. This figure may, however, be an overestimate as it is based mainly on returns from large socialized enterprises. It may not, therefore, adequately reflect the rapid growth of smaller state enterprises and the private sector. Key elements in the output decline were the drought and the large fall in the volume of ruble exports (about 30 percent). Personal consumption declined by more than 10 percent in real terms, and private saving rose to record levels. Despite depressed domestic demand, inflation rose to nearly 30 percent. The higher-than-forecast inflation resulted partly from the effects of the mid-year corrective fiscal package, from the drought, and from higher oil prices. Tight financial policies also had less impact in bringing down inflation than initially hoped.

The Government's Medium-Term Program

In the fall of 1990, the Government adopted a comprehensive medium-term program designed to put in place the most important elements, including the institutional framework, of a contemporary market economy within three years. The Government aims to construct a modern European social market economy, integrated into the world economy and emphasizing private property. On the basis of this reform program, the IMF approved in February 1991 an extended arrangement for $1.6 billion over three years. In addition, IMF financial support (of up to $0.5 billion) was provided to cover the increased cost of oil imports. In March 1991, the Government launched a four-year Action Program for Stabilization and Convertibility.

The Government is committed to reducing the State's role in the economy through privatization and other measures, strengthening the operation of the free market, and through the development of an adequate social safety net. Its strategic aim is to create a social market economy. The reform measures undertaken and proposed—which provided the basis of the current agreement with the IMF on an extended facility—are described in detail in earlier sections. Briefly, the Government's goal is to achieve a decline in state-owned property to less than half total assets in the competitive sphere of the economy by 1993. Foreign investment is to be encouraged. A radical transformation of public finances—including lower subsidies—is key to reducing the State's role in the economy. Competition will be strengthened by the major liberalization of both prices and imports, which occurred at the beginning of 1991, as well as by the establishment of a Cartel Office. Loss-making enterprises will continue to be restructured or closed, with the process accelerated by a new bankruptcy law. The banking system will be subject to prudential supervision conforming to international standards, and monetary policy will rely increasingly on market-based instruments. A major reform of social assistance is under way; the reform seeks to improve the targeting of social benefits to those in greatest need and to strengthen job retraining and unemployment compensation programs. Environmental deterioration will be checked through the promotion of greater energy efficiency, which, in turn, will entail appropriate pricing and taxation and the control of pollution through fees, fines, and other measures. The Government attaches priority to improving the education system—with emphasis on higher education and better language training—and fostering research and development as key for improving the long-term competitiveness of the economy.

A crucial element of the program is tight financial and budgetary policies aimed at regulating domestic demand. The switch, from 1991 on, to trading with CMEA partners at world prices presents Hungary with a major uncertainty. A large terms of trade loss results as export prices of manufactures decline relative to import prices of raw materials—notably oil and energy products. While Hungary and the U.S.S.R. have agreed that Hungary's accumulated surpluses with the U.S.S.R. of about $1 billion will be converted to U.S. dollars at the exchange rate of $0.92 per transferable ruble, no agreement has been reached on when these surpluses can be used. Preliminary first-quarter results in 1991 show a sharp contraction in trade with the Soviet Union. Various other shocks are affecting the Hungarian economy in 1991—notably higher world oil prices (at least temporarily) and the continuing effects of the drought. These shocks together imply a significant worsening of the convertible current account and of the fiscal deficit. Together with industrial restructuring, they imply a further fall in output and a rise in unemployment over the medium term.

The immediate goal of policies in 1991 is to ensure that both the external and fiscal accounts adjust to one half of the shocks outlined above, while curtailing inflation. Thus, financial policies for 1991 have been designed to limit the budget deficit to $1^1/_2$ percent of GDP, allowing the flow of more financial resources to the productive sector of the economy. The growth in money supply will be tailored to limiting the rate of inflation (after corrective price adjustments) to about 30 percent, while ensuring that credit is available to the enterprise sector, particularly private enterprises. Progress in reducing inflation is expected to be slow as subsidies continue to be reduced, other economic reforms are introduced, and increases in energy costs are passed through to consumers. The forint was depreciated by 15 percent in January 1991 to preserve external competitiveness.

The Government's medium-term objective is to reduce inflation to single digits by 1993. It also aims to maintain Hungary's traditional access to capital markets by halting the growth of external indebtedness within three years. The Government's approach to debt management remains guided by the principle that, given a realistic amount of external support, Hungary will fully and promptly comply with its international payment obligations. Over the medium term, the Government hopes to achieve an annual economic growth rate of at least 5 percent. The Government believes that the development of an internationally efficient economy, in the context of financial and budgetary policies effectively regulating domestic demand, represents the best prospect for attaining such a level of sustainable growth.

The Hungarian Government elected in spring 1990 inherited an onerous legacy of excessive state intervention, environmental degradation, and large external debt. It also inherited a well-educated labor force and considerable progress in certain areas of reform. The Government is seeking to tackle this legacy and build on these advantages through its medium-term reform program. The reward is clear: Hungary's growth potential—from a relatively low base—is large.

Recent Occasional Papers of the International Monetary Fund

83. Economic Reform in Hungary Since 1968, by Anthony R. Boote and Janos Somogyi. 1991.
82. Characteristics of a Successful Exchange Rate System, by Jacob A. Frenkel, Morris Goldstein, and Paul R. Masson. 1991.
81. Currency Convertibility and the Transformation of Centrally Planned Economies, by Joshua E. Greene and Peter Isard. 1991.
80. Domestic Public Debt of Externally Indebted Countries, by Pablo E. Guidotti and Manmohan S. Kumar. 1991.
79. The Mongolian People's Republic: Toward a Market Economy, by Elizabeth Milne, John Leimone, Franek Rozwadowski, and Padej Sukachevin. 1991.
78. Exchange Rate Policy in Developing Countries: Some Analytical Issues, by Bijan B. Aghevli, Mohsin S. Khan, and Peter J. Montiel. 1991.
77. Determinants and Systemic Consequences of International Capital Flows, by Morris Goldstein, Donald J. Mathieson, David Folkerts-Landau, Timothy Lane, J. Saúl Lizondo, and Liliana Rojas-Suárez. 1991.
76. China: Economic Reform and Macroeconomic Management, by Mario Blejer, David Burton, Steven Dunaway, and Gyorgy Szapary. 1991.
75. German Unification: Economic Issues, edited by Leslie Lipschitz and Donogh McDonald. 1990.
74. The Impact of the European Community's Internal Market on the EFTA, by Richard K. Abrams, Peter K. Cornelius, Per L. Hedfors, and Gunnar Tersman. 1990.
73. The European Monetary System: Developments and Perspectives, by Horst Ungerer, Jouko J. Hauvonen, Augusto Lopez-Claros, and Thomas Mayer. 1990.
72. The Czech and Slovak Federal Republic: An Economy in Transition, by Jim Prust and an IMF Staff Team. 1990.
71. MULTIMOD Mark II: A Revised and Extended Model, by Paul Masson, Steven Symansky, and Guy Meredith. 1990.
70. The Conduct of Monetary Policy in the Major Industrial Countries: Instruments and Operating Procedures, by Dallas S. Batten, Michael P. Blackwell, In-Su Kim, Simon E. Nocera, and Yuzuru Ozeki. 1990.
69. International Comparisons of Government Expenditure Revisited: The Developing Countries, 1975–86, by Peter S. Heller and Jack Diamond. 1990.
68. Debt Reduction and Economic Activity, by Michael P. Dooley, David Folkerts-Landau, Richard D. Haas, Steven A. Symansky, and Ralph W. Tryon. 1990.
67. The Role of National Saving in the World Economy: Recent Trends and Prospects, by Bijan B. Aghevli, James M. Boughton, Peter J. Montiel, Delano Villanueva, and Geoffrey Woglom. 1990.
66. The European Monetary System in the Context of the Integration of European Financial Markets, by David Folkerts-Landau and Donald J. Mathieson. 1989.
65. Managing Financial Risks in Indebted Developing Countries, by Donald J. Mathieson, David Folkerts-Landau, Timothy Lane, and Iqbal Zaidi. 1989.
64. The Federal Republic of Germany: Adjustment in a Surplus Country, by Leslie Lipschitz, Jeroen Kremers, Thomas Mayer, and Donogh McDonald. 1989.
63. Issues and Developments in International Trade Policy, by Margaret Kelly, Naheed Kirmani, Miranda Xafa, Clemens Boonekamp, and Peter Winglee. 1988.
62. The Common Agricultural Policy of the European Community: Principles and Consequences, by Julius Rosenblatt, Thomas Mayer, Kasper Bartholdy, Dimitrios Demekas, Sanjeev Gupta, and Leslie Lipschitz. 1988.

61. Policy Coordination in the European Monetary System. Part I: The European Monetary System: A Balance Between Rules and Discretion, by Manuel Guitián. Part II: Monetary Coordination Within the European Monetary System: Is There a Rule? by Massimo Russo and Giuseppe Tullio. 1988.

60. Policies for Developing Forward Foreign Exchange Markets, by Peter J. Quirk, Graham Hacche, Viktor Schoofs, and Lothar Weniger. 1988.

59. Measurement of Fiscal Impact: Methodological Issues, edited by Mario I. Blejer and Ke-Young Chu. 1988.

58. The Implications of Fund-Supported Adjustment Programs for Poverty: Experiences in Selected Countries, by Peter S. Heller, A. Lans Bovenberg, Thanos Catsambas, Ke-Young Chu, and Parthasarathi Shome. 1988.

57. The Search for Efficiency in the Adjustment Process: Spain in the 1980s, by Augusto Lopez-Claros. 1988.

56. Privatization and Public Enterprises, by Richard Hemming and Ali M. Mansoor. 1988.

55. Theoretical Aspects of the Design of Fund-Supported Adjustment Programs: A Study by the Research Department of the International Monetary Fund. 1987.

54. Protection and Liberalization: A Review of Analytical Issues, by W. Max Corden. 1987.

53. Floating Exchange Rates in Developing Countries: Experience with Auction and Interbank Markets, by Peter J. Quirk, Benedicte Vibe Christensen, Kyung-Mo Huh, and Toshihiko Sasaki. 1987.

52. Structural Reform, Stabilization, and Growth in Turkey, by George Kopits. 1987.

51. The Role of the SDR in the International Monetary System: Studies by the Research and Treasurer's Departments of the International Monetary Fund. 1987.

50. Strengthening the International Monetary System: Exchange Rates, Surveillance, and Objective Indicators, by Andrew Crockett and Morris Goldstein. 1987.

49. Islamic Banking, by Zubair Iqbal and Abbas Mirakhor. 1987.

48. The European Monetary System: Recent Developments, by Horst Ungerer, Owen Evans, Thomas Mayer, and Philip Young. 1986.

47. Aging and Social Expenditure in the Major Industrial Countries, 1980–2025, by Peter S. Heller, Richard Hemming, Peter W. Kohnert, and a Staff Team from the Fiscal Affairs Department. 1986.

46. Fund-Supported Programs, Fiscal Policy, and Income Distribution: A Study by the Fiscal Affairs Department of the International Monetary Fund. 1986.

45. Switzerland's Role as an International Financial Center, by Benedicte Vibe Christensen. 1986.

44. A Review of the Fiscal Impulse Measure, by Peter S. Heller, Richard D. Haas, and Ahsan H. Mansur. 1986.

42. Global Effects of Fund-Supported Adjustment Programs, by Morris Goldstein. 1986.

41. Fund-Supported Adjustment Programs and Economic Growth, by Mohsin S. Kahn and Malcolm D. Knight. 1985.

39. A Case of Successful Adjustment: Korea's Experience During 1980–84, by Bijan B. Aghevli and Jorge Márquez-Ruarte. 1985.

38. Trade Policy Issues and Developments, by Shailendra J. Anjaria, Naheed Kirmani, and Arne B. Petersen. 1985.

Note: For information on the title and availability of Occasional Papers not listed, please consult the IMF *Publications Catalog* or contact IMF Publication Services. Occasional Paper Nos. 5–26 are $5.00 a copy (academic rate: $3.00); Nos. 27–64 are $7.50 a copy (academic rate: $4.50); and from No. 65 on, the price is $10.00 a copy (academic rate: $7.50).